LEGLESS
TO
LEGLESS

LEGLESS TO LEGLESS

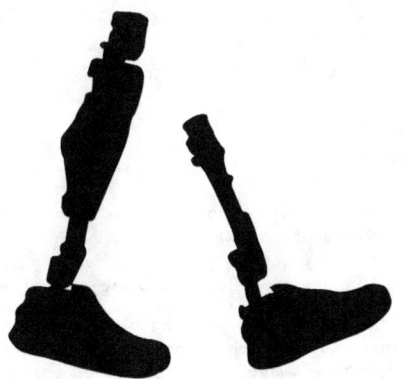

THE **KHOA NAM TRAN** STORY

First published in 2020 by Dean Publishing
PO Box 119
Mt. Macedon, Victoria, 3441
Australia
deanpublishing.com

Copyright © Khoa Nam Tran

All rights reserved. No part of this publication may be reproduced, stored in a retrieval system or transmitted in any way or by any means, electronic, mechanical, photocopying, recording or otherwise, without the prior written permission of the publisher.

Cataloguing-in-Publication Data
National Library of Australia
Title: Legless to Legless: The Khoa Nam Tran Story
Edition: 1st edn
ISBN: 978-1-925452-29-7
Category: Memoir/self-help

This is an autobiography, the author has tried to recreate events, locales and conversations from his memories of them. In order to maintain anonymity of certain individuals in some instances names, occupations and places have been changed to protect individuals. Certain identifying characteristics and details such as physical properties, occupations and places of residence may have changed.

This book is a personal memoir and not intended as a substitute for the medical advice of physicians. The reader should regularly consult a physician in matters relating to his/her health and particularly with respect to any symptoms that may require diagnosis or medical attention. This is not intended for medical purposes or promote any particular type of treatment than that recommended to the individual from their own medical team— each person is different.

The views and opinions expressed in this book are those of the authors and do not necessarily reflect the official policy or position of any other agency, publisher, organisation, medical team, employer or company. Assumptions made in the analysis are not reflective of the position of any entity other than the author(s) — and, these views are always subject to change, revision, and rethinking at any time.

The authors or organisations are not to be held responsible for misuse, reuse, recycled and cited and/or uncited copies of content within this book by others.

DEDICATION

I dedicate this book to you, the reader.

I'm sure you're going through your own challenges in this crazy journey of life. I've learnt that the hurdles can make you stronger and braver to face the unknown adventures ahead and I want to pass this hope onto you too. The personal challenges that I'm about to share with you when you flip over to the next page will inspire you to stand tall and sail over your own; so buckle up and enjoy the ride!

I truly hope it makes you smile.

CONTENTS

Chapter 1 **FREEDOM FIRST** 9

Chapter 2 **THRILLS AND SPILLS** 25

Chapter 3 **HAZARD AHEAD** 47

Chapter 4 **ROLLERCOASTER TO RECOVERY** ... 67

Chapter 5 **THE SLOW LANE** 91

Chapter 6 **GO GO GADGET LEGS** 113

Chapter 7 **LEVELLING UP** 153

Chapter 8 **LEGLESS TO LEGLESS** 173

Khoa's Five Life Lessons 191

Acknowledgements 194

About the author 196

Testimonials 197

End notes 199

> The life you live now doesn't cement your future, it only gives you a sneak peek into your potential.

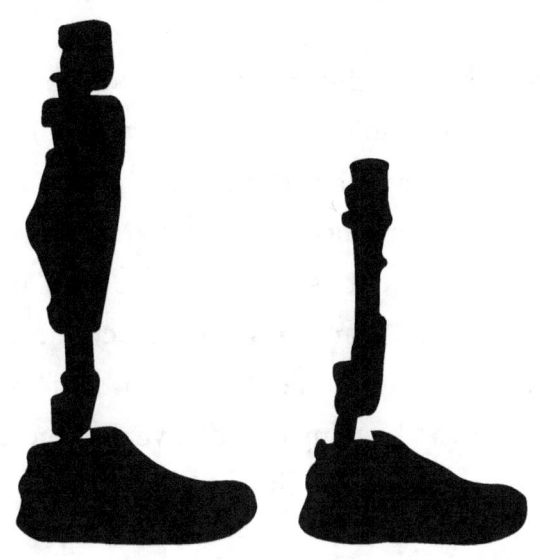

CHAPTER 1
FREEDOM FIRST

B orn smiling and born fast, that was me. Mum said the nurse barely caught me. Life doesn't wait for you after all. I've always enjoyed the speed of life and finding the brighter side to any situation.

I rarely slow down or look back and I'm not really a details guy but my life today is not something I could have ever predicted. Who would've thought I'd be built like a T800 Terminator saving the day one smile at a time? Yet I

CHAPTER 1

know I'm only here in this great place today because of the lessons from my past, so let's put the brake on for a minute to see what kicked off my mad adventure.

I've been smiling since I was a kid growing up amid the smell of hot pork rolls in the jungle of Cabramatta, a patchwork suburb of Asian and European cultures southwest of Sydney. Growing up in the '90s it wasn't safe to go out at night. By day it was a bustling hive of diversity and commerce, by night it was business of a different kind.

The heart of Cabramatta and the Vietnamese capital in Australia, which has the world's best hot chips and fried chicken.

Good old Cabra' had the proud title of being the drug capital of Australia. The only late night shops were the pork roll shops whose busiest trade was after dark. Those bread rolls coming fresh out of the oven at 2am are still to die for.

I'm a first generation Australian; both my parents lived on the south coast of Vietnam but only met each other when they had to flee as refugees after the war ended in 1975. The advancing communist government from the north made life difficult and dangerous for many people. So hundreds of thousands of Vietnamese people in the south took their chances and escaped on boats desperate to find a free life somewhere across the sea.

Mum was one of 104 people crammed onto a small wooden boat only 11m long. I can't imagine her desperation to escape on such a dangerous journey. Even the captain couldn't handle it. He had a panic attack and aborted his own vessel moments after it departed.

With no captain on-board, one of the passengers had to pilot the ship without any navigational skills. As long as their homeland kept disappearing behind them, they felt safe. This feeling didn't last. Thai pirates attacked their boat four times, ransacking personal belongings and separating the women from the men to do unimaginable things.

Unfortunately this was a common story for the nearly one million refugees that continued to flee Vietnam for

CHAPTER 1

many years after the war ended.[1] Boat people battled storms, diseases, starvation, pirates and the constant risk of sinking; many thousands died at sea. My parents were lucky to survive.

On the 11th day of Mum's escape she had thought they were rescued when a Thai Navy vessel appeared. However they didn't want to rescue anyone, they only supplied a bit of fuel. It was just enough for her boat to sail on to Malaysian waters. When the Malay Navy ships arrived, they escorted the boat onto a beach, where again Mum thought it would mean freedom at last.

She waited on the beach with 900 other refugees also found by the Malay Navy. However rescue was the last thing on those sailors' minds. They knew there'd still be valuables hidden in the refugees' boats that the pirates hadn't found.

So they ordered the refugees onto seven of the Navy's own boats; seven battered old boats even more unseaworthy than the one Mum originally escaped on. They were forced to board these death traps and the Navy simply towed them out to sea and left them there. With no fuel or food on board, they would surely die!

The sly game of the Malay Navy continued when they told the passengers that a French hospital ship, *Ile de Lumiere*, was departing Malaysia and would most likely intercept the seven vessels left drifting.

Most likely!

Their plan was to have the French ship rescue all 900 refugees from these death vessels and then retrieve their boats back: a win/win for the Malay Navy - right? Wrong!

Thankfully the French ship did pick up the refugees and once aboard the captain asked them to go below deck. After the French crew checked there was no one left behind on the decaying boats, they severely damaged the hulls of all the vessels. The potential deathbeds of 900 people sank into the depths.

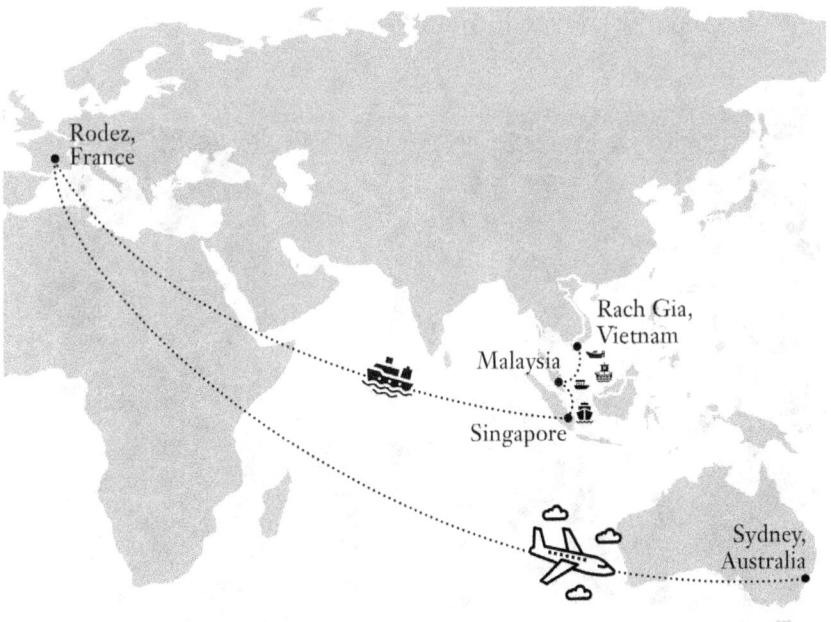

My parents' journey from their war-stricken homeland to eventually finding freedom in Australia.

CHAPTER 1

Ile de Lumiere quickly turned about to the open ocean on full throttle and raced towards Singapore. Arriving too late, the Malay Navy could do nothing but watch; the French were too far ahead for a chase. My mother's life had been saved.

From Singapore, Vietnamese refugees could apply for asylum from countries that offered resettlement for people who had escaped a war torn country. As her saviour in her most desperate hour, Mum chose France. She met Dad while en route to France to start a new beginning. My father had had a similarly turbulent journey yet was still one of the lucky ones to make it to freedom and safety.

My siblings and I in Paris on a rare holiday with Mum and Dad.

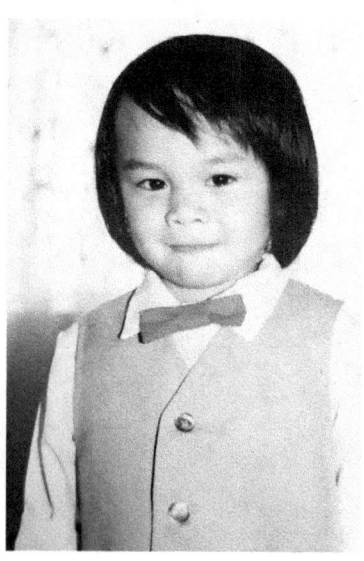

Forced to suit up to go to a dinner party.

My parents lived in Rodez in southern France for a few years and my siblings and I were born there. In 1985, we came to Australia on a sponsorship visa, as Mum's mother and brother were already here. I was only two years old. We settled in Cabramatta where my grandmother moved in with us and Mum and Dad found jobs doing sewing and factory work. They had found safety and opportunities for us all.

∿∿

I grew up an animal lover, everything from the fish in our homemade fishpond in the backyard, to the many dogs we had growing up and more recently to the seven stray cats we look after today. Tip — if you want to avoid stray cats coming to your house, don't put food in front of your house every day. Word of Mum's soft heart spread amongst the neighbourhood cats and they've been hanging around our house ever since. She's the cat lady, talk about a 'meow' symphony every time she opens the back door!

I always loved my bike and a bit of speed. We lived on a really steep driveway and all the local kids knew it was the best spot for cruising down the slope of the road and turning sharply into the incline of our driveway, giving you

CHAPTER 1

momentum to turn around and do it over and over again. We were little speed machines and have the scars to prove it.

Mum and Dad would take us to visit my uncle's family and it was great staying for sleepovers. We would turn on the Acer Intel Pentium 166 MMX, waiting for Windows 95 to load ('90s software taught me patience) and play games like Solitaire and Grand Theft Auto. If they got boring, we would run downstairs to play Alex Kidd on the Sega Master System. Computer games formed a great bond between cousins. We were small for a Vietnamese family but we were close.

We grew up as Buddhists but enjoyed the celebration of Christmas too, which meant family, food and presents. As a kid, I didn't connect Christmas with a religion; it was just cool and exciting waiting for presents. I loved dressing up and feeling wise once a year putting on that white beard.

Another tradition I looked forward to was Chinese New Year when our relatives would give us the traditional 'red pockets' with money in them as a way to wish good wealth upon us. As you know I only had one uncle so I couldn't help noticing how many relatives other kids had.

I was lucky if I could afford a few school lunches with my red pocket money. I was always envious that my friends collected enough money to buy computer games. I would have to save and save to afford a game; I guess it made me more appreciative of money because it was earned, not given.

My mum, sister and me looking extremely cute.

L–R, cameo by my half sister (full of mysteries aren't I 😊), my sister, me, my brother, my grandma and my mum celebrating my birthday… I think it's mine ha ha.

CHAPTER 1

Heading off to the Sydney Easter Show each year was another highlight; the buzz of the atmosphere, the packed crowds of the Show Bag Hall, thinking you were outsmarting the seller by getting the 2 for 1 discount, ha ha!

I was one of those thrill-seeking kids going on all the rides. Not the spinning rides though, unless you wanted to see the day's lunch special again in mashed form. I loved everything else but especially the bumper cars. No stunts were off limits once you were flying around that electric track - *Mario Kart* anyone? Minus loose banana peels and red turtle shells.

Mum and Dad worked really hard for us. Dad worked on the production line of a cardboard factory and Mum either sewed at home or sometimes in a warehouse. We didn't really go on holidays. In primary school we visited family friends in Newcastle and Wollongong but didn't go anywhere when I was in high school; I made the hours after school and the weekend my holidays.

My parents were quite strict. Dad was a Shaolin Master, an ancient martial art that follows strict disciplines. Like many Asian cultures, Vietnamese place great value on respecting our elders and ancestors; this tradition is supposed to help create well-behaved children. Not surprisingly my antics often fell a little short of expectations.

Like the time I wanted to see what would happen if I lit a match and pushed it into my dad's surround sound speakers

— he had a thing for good sound. I watched the mesh oozing and melting thinking it was so cool, but boy, was he mad when he got home! He made me kneel on the floor and face the corner, which for me was torture, looking at that boring plaster wall for an hour was agony to a mind and body that was always desperate for movement and adventure.

∿∿

A little creek ran behind our house. We used to dash over a fallen log that acted as a bridge and my friends and I would go tadpoling in the creek's clear water (fast forward 25 years and it's now murky with stolen cars sunk into the mud, handy as habitat for any fish that might have survived the toxic odds) or we'd play in the streets: handball, shuttlecock, marbles or riding around on bikes as we got older.

Back then, there were open, undeveloped areas all around us. Our neighbourhood was full of backyard vegie patches and orchards. My mates and I were the neighbourhood rascals and would dare each other to steal juicy oranges and mandarins from the backfields in summer. We'd pedal slowly down the alleyways towards the bigger properties, planning our raid.

CHAPTER 1

The chosen thief would rest his bike up against the fence and creep bravely into action by sneaking over the fence. The rest of us would be lookouts. The hard bit was deciding how far away to wait; the further away you waited, the bigger chicken you were. Yet if the owner spotted us and came out yelling, you wanted to be the furthest away because it became every man for himself!

In our mad dash to escape someone might get a flat tyre or a bike chain would slip off but we'd just ruin the wheel as we all pedalled like bats out of hell, our hearts racing! No one wanted a walloping from the owner; there weren't any laws against that back then and no such thing as political correctness.

I didn't know it at the time but a few things strike me now as being special about my neighbourhood. My mates and I could all walk or ride to each other's houses. Every day we felt a sense of connection, belonging and opportunity for fun.

We all loved video games. From Super Nintendo's Mario Kart and Donkey Kong Country to Nintendo 64 Ocarina of Time and GoldenEye 007. Those consoles kept us grounded and focused, and there was much happiness when we played together (aside from the crick in the neck we'd feel sometimes from looking down — roll on those smartphones please).

They weren't internet games; you had to go to someone's house to play. That's where the connection was: playing, laughing, eating snacks together. It's funny thinking back to when there was no NBN, only dialup. You had to yell at your family to get off the phone when you wanted to use the internet; I loved the buzzing jingle tone as it connected.

I've always loved technology but never thought one day I would literally need it to walk.

Mostly as kids, fun was found outside in the air and sunshine. We spent hours every chance we could riding around the neighbourhood exploring or coming up with crazy plans. After school we would ride to the park where my friends and I had built a bike track hidden behind the bushes.

It felt awesome flying over the homemade ramps of scrub, rocks and wood, anything we could find. It was no good in the rain but once the sun dried it up, it was race time. Most of all, it was our private world with no adults in sight.

I still have the scar from when I hit the deck being doubled by my brother on his bike. As we skidded around the corner I came off the handlebars and scraped my arms along the road. I limped to the footpath and saw my arm was basically loose meat and pebbles. Gross! The skin was torn off and took ages to heal but it didn't stop me for long.

Moments like that showed me that I was a pretty tough cookie. I could never have envisaged this pathway I'm on now but I guess they're all pieces of the pie that my mad adventures would ultimately cook up.

CHAPTER 1

I used to love taking my bike apart and seeing how all the mechanics worked. They were pretty generic bikes so I'd look at each part and see how I could juice it up a bit, from getting a gyro and anodised brake levers to even getting those little dice-looking valve caps. I would change the tyres to slicks to give it more speed, except if it was wet — forget it, slippery as hell unless you liked aquaplaning on a glossy surface for a

One of my favourite pastimes, hitting the trails. You can't tell that I'm standing next to a sheer drop off and my heart is thumping.

little out of control, heart-in-your-mouth fun.

From that time spent in the backyard covered in bike grease and reading *Hot4s* and *Wheels Magazine* my love of mechanics has never stopped. You've gotta love the centrefold of girls posing in front of hot cars (no - not *those* centrefolds 😊).

Looking back I can also see what a melting pot of cultures my neighbourhood was. Cabramatta High School was probably the most multicultural high school in the country. Vietnamese, Chinese, Indian, Serbian, Croatian, Italian and the rare token white Aussie. That didn't matter to me though; my mates could be white or brown or black, I didn't care. We had our groups but anyone could join mine if they liked my jokes enough.

I found that a mate was a mate in the way he treated you, not what he looked like. I gave them no rankings, had no best friend; they were all my mates. I think they liked that I always found the lighter side of things to make people laugh. They knew where to come if they wanted a laugh and a smile.

Khoa is sharing more in his INTERACTIVE book.

See exclusive videos, audios and photos.

DOWNLOAD it now at
deanpublishing.com/legless

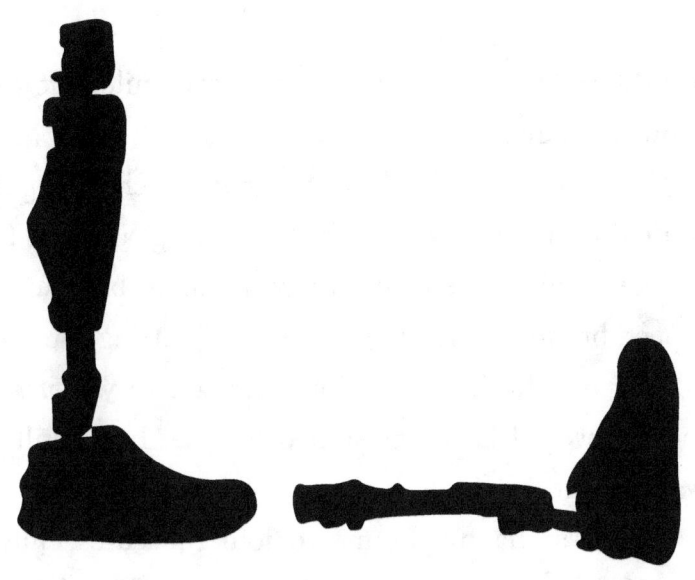

CHAPTER 2
THRILLS AND SPILLS

School was fun for me, like a social experiment; I could test out my jokes all day. I kept decent grades for a few years: computers and information technology were my thing. Would you believe I was even selected as a prefect? Or was it for the Year 8 committee? Oh I forget the details.

The point is, it was being cool in a nerdy way and I always wondered why I got picked because I know for sure I did not contribute to anything worthy back then, hah! I was

CHAPTER 2

very likeable though so it had to be my smile that got me the brownie points .

I knew plenty of kids who jigged off school regularly and wanted to be seen as the cool kids taking risks but I only did it once. I told myself I didn't worry about being cool in that aspect, but more likely I was afraid of getting caught because I knew that having detention after school was *not* what my mother would have envisioned for me. I can still hear her warning me, "I didn't raise you to be a brat!"

She was happy for me to join the chess club though. "OMG, the chess club?" I hear you say, "That's so nerdy of you!" Why yes, you could see it that way, or I could explain that the club travelled to other schools for competitions which took hours out of my normal school day. See what I did there? Everyone was happy.

I actually ended up really loving chess and still do. In 2019 I had the pleasure of watching Garry Kasparov on stage in Los Angeles playing four people at once while getting questioned by the audience. He could calculate the endless possibilities of the game at least eight steps ahead of his competition. How incredible are our minds, so powerful.

THRILLS AND SPILLS

In high school I was also an opportunist. A guy I knew came into mysterious possession 😊, of a Fujitsu CD writer. This machine was a big deal at the time because not many people had one yet and I wanted to be the first in the school. So I haggled a good price and bought it from the guy so I could make music CDs to sell to people.

They'd request songs; I'd compile and burn them onto CD. Back then the read/write speeds were written as 4x/2x; 4times read, 2times write, and that was when CD-R just came out. I would spend a good couple hours (I know, how prehistoric) burning 8 songs onto a 650MB CD. This put me at the forefront of technology at our school for a while, hot stuff.

I was planning on going to university after school but as I hit Year 11, life wasn't quite going to plan. My parents

My Fabio phase in high school with my usual partners in crime, it's better if you don't know what we got up to 😊.

CHAPTER 2

split up, Dad moved out and my grades slipped a lot. I still don't know if the build-up towards my parents' divorce was the reason I didn't try as hard, or I was happy to *use* it as the reason not to try as hard and slack off a bit.

Even the seed of possibility that I did use that as an excuse has motivated me to try and be the polar opposite ever since. I allow myself no excuses for anything now - just go for it! I've been nurturing that philosophy for over twenty years where there is no room for regrets.

After Dad moved out, I knew I had to help out and support my mum. She was a great seamstress, working between home and the warehouse when they needed her. She worked hard but it didn't pay well and the bills and mortgage would have been a struggle. Holidays were a luxury we couldn't afford and even those occasional visits to friends along the coast dried up altogether in high school.

So instead of university I looked for a job straight away. It just so happened that Burger King was opening a new restaurant near my house and they were looking for workers. *Yes*, I thought, *how perfect*. A job that was only a ten-minute walk from home and could feed my family for free.

Hey! Don't judge me for taking home excess 'waste'. Someone's gotta eat those five Whoppers and lonely Bacon Deluxe burger sitting on the chute after closing time. I know what you're thinking. Did I make extra burgers on purpose?

THRILLS AND SPILLS

Damn straight I did! My stomach was a bottomless pit at that age.

I was asked to be the manager but I declined, I didn't want to stay in the job too long and probably wasn't ready for the extra responsibilities anyway. Being the kitchen hand suited me fine, I just had to make burgers and clean, make burgers and clean. Occasionally the manager checked something with me, but even that was rare, as they knew I took my position seriously.

One of my kitchen buddies challenged us to see who could make the fastest Whopper. Yes, it was *I* who triumphed over those amateurs with a speedy time of 20 seconds from the toasting to the wrapping. I felt like Speedy Gonzales stealing cheese off Sylvester the Cat with a smirk; a race is a race after all.

I was happy being the broiler boy, putting the patties through the furnace; I kept it really clean and other franchisees would ask for tips on how I kept it so clean. I always believed no matter what work you do, don't take shortcuts, and do it as well as you can with passion.

I would give most of my wage to Mum and keep a little for myself. Food wasn't a problem as you might have gathered. The next few years I was just happy to be supporting Mum and I didn't think about saving for the future or anything like that. My mindset at the time was to have a roof to live under

CHAPTER 2

and to pass on most of my wage to Mum. This surely did help relieve a lot of her financial stress.

∿∿∿

I didn't touch a drop of alcohol until I was 18, after I finished high school. I admit I took to it like a duck to water and I pretty much worked for the weekends. I loved that rush of total freedom and acceptance with everyone in that same state of being: happily drunk. Fridays and Saturdays were a reward for the hard work throughout the week.

There'd be a party at my house with drinking and karaoke until all hours. Belting out Bon Jovi's "Always" with friends as we swayed and sang our hearts out, was a bonding experience. (I still don't get why she cheated on him with the artist guy in the music video ... oh wait, that's right, *he* cheated on her first - go figure.)

I started going out with a girl I worked with, she liked to drink and party too and was part of my close group of friends. A weekly cycle of *work, party, drink, repeat* began. While it was fun, now I realise it was a cycle that didn't offer any potential for growth. Hindsight is a wonderful thing isn't it?

A big part of our weekend scene was going to the 'runs'

on a Saturday night. Street races were part of the Sydney suburban sub-culture back then. They'd start around 10pm and go until 2 or 3 in the morning. I was obsessed seeing those cars with all their high performance mods and dazzled up looks, there was virtually a new conversion to marvel over each week or a pumped up car you were waiting to see run.

From Nissan Skylines with loud exhausts hearing the turbos spool and expel engine gases with a high-pitched blow off valve turned everyone's heads; to the sex spec cars like the Subaru WRX with their candy apple red glitter paint jobs with lowered 21inch chrome wheels to make any girl orgasm with its sheer stance presence.

Meanwhile I'd turn up to the runs in Mum's little green Camry. Yeah, it was a typical Asian family car around Cabramatta, but I had an aftermarket exhaust installed to stand out from the crowd, aka ricer spec. This means no functional purpose; it's just for looks but still drives like a nugget. I was still a poor burger flipper remember.

Even finding the runs could be a challenge. Word would go around where the cars were going to race and you just prayed it was true. They'd often use a decoy venue so as groups of people would gather in one street waiting for the cars, the real races were already happening a mile away for those few in the know: the bigger the crowd, the more likely to attract the red and blue. If you did get duped, your Saturday night could just

CHAPTER 2

end up as a bunch of people hanging around: a real bummer.

As time went on and the police became more vigilant of illegal racing, it was even harder to know where the real races were going to be. I decided I'd have to befriend some guys who were regulars of the runs so I used my biggest smile to earn a call from them with the real deal. Sometimes the call would come through when I was at the decoy runs and it felt like I had to go undercover and try to act natural while a few of my friends and I would slink away.

I didn't want to make a sudden move that would spark any notice. That's like the kid who screams, "Ice cream van!" to a park full of kids and then misses out when they all race over. In this case, if the crowd followed me, the police would notice the crowd and it would be over before it began. Occasionally the police would hit onto the races and over the roar of the engines someone would yell, "Cops!" and we'd all scatter like mice with our hearts thumping.

In 2003 I still couldn't afford my own car but my brother and I were pretty impressed with ourselves when we talked Mum into upgrading the Camry to a Nissan Skyline. The Japanese

THRILLS AND SPILLS

The infamous Skyline—aka The Black Beast—lovingly spec'd up to satisfy my need for speed until she fell apart from exhaustion.

import cars were huge at the time; they were affordable sporty streetcars. It didn't take long for me to have my third accident with it.

"*Third? What were the first two?*" Thank you for asking — let me recap.

I had my first accident only two weeks after getting my P plates (still in high school) and while that car was getting repaired they gave me a courtesy car to drive and yes — you guessed it — I had a second accident with the courtesy car too!

I clearly remember going home to Mum and ripping up

CHAPTER 2

my licence, swearing never to drive again, I was devastated at what I had done. I hadn't been hooning, just a bit thoughtless and it ended up costing me a lot. Makes for a funny story now though.

Fast forward a couple of years to lucky accident number three. *Ah yes*, we think we know it all when we're young but we don't do we? I'm not proud to admit that I might have, possibly, sort of, made up a little story that I had hit a pothole, when in actual fact I had been attempting to drift but the car ended up spinning out and hitting the gutter! Talk about hero to zero in two seconds. I had no money and couldn't afford to fix it so had to play the pity card. *Not sure if you know this yet do you Mum? Sorry!*

Once we had the Skyline, I started going to the National Park runs. A bunch of us car enthusiasts would meet up at Macca's and head out to the National Parks around Sydney. It was still underground racing but was even more exciting because of the nature of the Parks' tracks, the twists and turns of the gravel roads were akin to rally driving but these were held at night!

High beams were the only safety requirement; it was still a public two-way, single lane road. It was one of the ways I liked to live on the edge; there was only a railing to stop you from going over the cliff face!

There was also a good chance of wildlife jumping out at

you; you could be smashed by a deer or a wallaby. My friends took a few big stacks, overestimating their ability to tackle turns at high speeds and screeching all four tyres into the guardrails: an expensive night out. We were at least an hour away from Sydney and I tell you, we did not want to pay for a tow truck out there in the middle of the night but it did happen.

Originally the Skyline was automatic, mainly for Mum but it slowly became a 'family' car and then my brother's and my car. I found a cheap manual gearbox that was in good nick so I knew what had to happen - conversion time. I felt a bit guilty that we had taken over the Skyline, so I ended up buying my mother another Skyline, it was an older model but we made sure that one stayed automatic for her.

I was heavily involved in the Skyline forums back before Facebook was invented, and being a money conscious guy, I did a lot of research before I attempted to do this gearbox swap. Let me tell you, lots of sweat and tears went into this project, from sourcing the correct parts to installing the manual pedal system while the car was still automatic. It was so satisfying undertaking this project myself which also saved me thousands of dollars in the long run.

The mechanic simply had to take the automatic gearbox out and install the manual gearbox. All his potential labour was negated by my preparation. I documented the process onto the forums so people who wanted to do a conversion could

CHAPTER 2

follow my 'How-to'. It's a shame that the photos I took of the work were lost (on a web server that I ended up forgetting to pay for — whoops) so now when I visit my 'How-to', it's just text with a broken image link, *doh!* Don't you hate when that happens, a picture tells a thousand words after all. Once it was converted to manual I took the car to the National Park runs, and then over time I'd head to the tracks, such as Wakefield Park Racetrack in Goulburn.

By this time I was working at Sydney airport as a labourer so I could afford to pay for a bit of track time. I was also wising up to the unpredictable costs of underground racing and the paranoia of cops waiting to pounce on you. Paying for track use in a controlled environment seemed a smarter choice; safer than battling loose gravel and wild creatures ambushing you.

My passion for all things mechanical helped me to convince my mate to let me work on his car. He wasn't a pure car enthusiast but he knew a nice looking car when he saw one. It was another project that I took the time to really focus on. The deal was I could work on his car, and he'd end up with a better car. Did I mention that he was one of the guys who hit the guardrails on one of our many runs? The car was already ruined so he might as well let me put my greasy fingers on it and fix it. It worked out well for him because I basically turned a 1989 model car into a modern spec interior '02 car. With a newish motor, a new rear cradle and a manual conversion, I basically changed half of the car's DNA. When I have a vision, I go for it.

ᴨᴜᴜ

Another interest I found around this time was photography. My dad was an artistic bloke and had some cool photography equipment. I based my first digital camera purchase on what he had in the old film version. I moulded my love of cars with photography and that's how I started my passion for taking pictures. The elegance of the curves flowing through the car's design features, trying to capture it on a 6-megapixel camera was an art form to learn and develop. You don't just become a photographer without practice. I can't imagine how many rolls I would have wasted during my trial practising with the DSLR.

My friends and I actually still loved bike riding too. We had moved on from pushbikes and now it was all about mountain biking. They were more work, more expensive but now we had full shock suspension to tackle the thrills of the jumps and obstacles and downhills. We'd research bike tracks on the internet and head out on the weekend to the great

CHAPTER 2

places around Sydney like Manly Dam.

It was at least an hour away from where I lived but boy was it worth the drive. An 11km circuit encompassing tarmac, gravel, dirt, grass, big rocks and hills that made you think twice about the value of your life. I had to pump my weedy legs like mad to make it around safely. We took video cameras just to record people stacking.

That track had it all for a brutal yet equally enjoyable day out. It was fitness plus action. Although I must confess, we would sometimes go to the local KFC right after for a well-deserved feed. Counter productive I know, but how can you say no to Hot & Spicy Chicken - it's Hot & Spicy!

I couldn't escape the dangers of these adventures forever. I had a bad stack on another trail on the outskirts of Sydney when I was 26. After many aborted attempts, I finally took a deep breath to tackle the last jump but misjudged the landing and smashed into a tree. Luckily I was wearing a full-face helmet that took the brunt of the impact.

I tore my knee up pretty badly and couldn't walk at all for weeks. But hey - my bike was still good. A few scuffmarks here and there to show for the story, a bit like my present self. It didn't stop me from getting back to mountain biking as soon as I was fit enough. The physical pain didn't really bother me. I guess that's where I got my perseverance from; after all no pain no gain.

My girlfriend and I had been dating for a good five years by that time and we planned to get married. We were all hunky-dory or so I thought when we headed out one night to a nightclub to have fun together with friends like we normally did.

But halfway through the night, something happened. A fight broke out and there were so many people scuffling around that I was lost as to what exactly was going on and who was involved. Was it one of us? Did they need help?

After all of this commotion came a confession that did not have to be. My mate (soon ex-mate, but now mate again) confessed out of confusion and presumption (and guilty conscience) that I knew what he was doing: that he had been hooking up with my fiancé!

Now I'm an easy going bloke and don't get caught up in that kind of drama but when I heard about my fiancé cheating on me with this good friend in our group, anger surged through me. I wanted to bash him! I didn't go through with it but I was so hurt and betrayed.

It's surprising to say it but I didn't want to throw away the future my fiancé and I had planned together so I thought

CHAPTER 2

about forgiving her. I actually tried to work it out. I knew I couldn't forgive him (at the time) but thought her and I might still make it. Fate decided otherwise though and she wanted to move on (now I say thank God!) and so I moved on too.

After the breakup, I didn't wait around and feel sorry for myself. I reconnected with some school buddies and let loose. It was fairly straightforward: work for the weekends and drink to get blind drunk. I was a bigger joker than ever and often the life of the party. It wasn't just karaoke at home anymore, we had started heading out to our favourite place, the Sugar Karaoke bar and then onto a club or a party somewhere. Vodka, gin, whisky and onto a sav blanc, I was no lightweight.

I felt this need for fun and freedom and adventure. I wanted to unwind from the last couple of years and let loose in the new direction my life could take now that marriage was off the cards. I felt like I'd been set free somehow, the house and white picket fence was something I never actually wanted anyway.

One thing my smile had always hidden was my fear of heights. Suddenly I wanted to face my fear head on so I decided to go skydiving in 2009 (I've done it with legs and without, that might be some sort of record). The moment when I finally had to shuffle to the edge of the open plane door with the instructor strapped to me had my heart bursting out of my chest! His instructions were simple; *head up, arms across your body and hope for the best*. I could do that.

The initial moment of weightlessness as I fell off the plane was the most exhilarating experience. Huge adrenaline as that rush of air hit me, slapping at my mouth and cheeks while I fell through the clouds. Through the scenery of mist, suddenly the world shot into focus, and I gained a bird's-eye view of the amazing landscape beneath me. The moment when the instructor pulled the chute, I was filled with appreciation and good fortune to be living on this beautiful earth.

I loved it so much I thought bungee jumping was the natural next step. Turns out it's definitely scarier than skydiving but I did it. Falling down alone with a bungee cord attached to me was frightening and thrilling at the same time; the buzz didn't stop until the bungee cord retracted back up. It's definitely a must do for anyone wanting to level up.

Next thing, a mate suggested we take off overseas for a while which was exactly where my need for adventure was at. Mum was doing okay by that time so I quit my airport job and spent two years travelling through Asia and a lot of South America. Seeing those countries gave me a new perspective on life. It showed me how privileged we are in Australia. I was amazed how clearly the line was between the 'haves' and the 'have nots'.

There was no gradual change between prosperity and poverty. The fortunate lived in the city high rises and then,

CHAPTER 2

tucked up hard against the walls of the last building, the tents and shacks of the slums began their sprawl out from the city. No one complained and I saw so many smiles; they just made do with their surroundings.

My mate and I didn't always travel together, just met up every few months so I could concentrate on my own thing. My interest in photography had grown since experimenting with photos of my cars. I had a great time testing out my equipment in the most amazing locations from Panama to Argentina.

I even got paid to be the photographer for a kite surfing school. I tried to learn kite surfing but was much better at

The slums on the outskirts of Cali in Colombia. A local showed me around and I meet some amazing characters.

taking the photos. I was able to work and move on quite a few times because cafés were often happy to employ someone who spoke English so I kept extending my return date.

I met so many friendly people over there. My endless rides in hostel elevators showed me how effective it is to smile and greet everyone as though you're about to be great friends. This might surprise you but alcohol wasn't a big part of my trip. I always kept in mind that I was still a foreigner in a strange land and so I didn't like to put all my eggs in one basket. I couldn't let my guard down completely with people I hadn't known very long and so I went months without drinking.

I changed my order at the bar to, *"Agua por favour?"* My Spanish was limited but got me through my time there. Just experiencing such different cultures and experimenting with my photography was really fulfilling without the need for alcohol.

I also became immersed in sport over there. Football games in Colombia are a test of bravery. The rivalry between teams for *El Clásico* is legendary and is taken more seriously than religion. Just imagine, two separate entries for fans at different times. First to be let in were the home club, Deportivo Cali fans and then their derby nemesis, América de Cali fans.

It was a tense standoff, police and security separated the

Panama. I loved the contrast between ancient and modern in one picture. The historical legacy of a country can never be forgotten.

two groups, ensuring they didn't mingle together and be tempted to throw fists or bottles or light flares and launch them at each other. It was very tense and when the game finished, it was a safety precaution not to wear your team's colours on the street and if you stumbled across any opposing fans, the best idea was not to make eye contact!

∿∿∿

It was a truly incredible trip and I returned at the start of 2012. I'd like to say I was older and wiser but only in certain ways. I was still ready to party anytime anywhere; I'd be there.

I hung out with a big group of extended friends and their friends and so on, people who all loved to party and would help each other find whatever was happening each weekend. Whoever put the party on would shout the alcohol so even though I didn't have any steady work, I could get by on my jokes and cheeky smile that let me in anywhere.

To be honest I still looked forward to drinking to the state of blindness every single time; I would vomit, recover and do it all again. Maybe I'd go to the gym if I were up to it the next day, to try and compensate for the night of drinking. Back then, that was my definition of being responsible.

CHAPTER 2

It is strange when I think about it now, my memory of these big nights out were often a total blank the next morning. My mates would have to fill me in on what happened when I woke up with a headache. They'd have to tell me about all the fun I'd had.

I had stepped up a notch and I didn't care what I drank; I'd mix my drinks all night, whatever was on offer. I was living only for the quick thrill of the party and was drinking harder than ever.

CHAPTER 3
HAZARD AHEAD

In early December of 2012, Christmas parties were in full swing and I'd enjoyed the festive season with a few hangovers already. I was living with a mate who knew I liked to party. Another Saturday night was coming up and I'd been invited to a girl's birthday party at a club I hadn't been to before, the Marquee nightclub at Sydney's Star Casino, sitting pretty in the hustle of Darling Harbour looking out over the water and city skyline.

CHAPTER 3

Think big-time gamblers chasing impossible money that inevitably goes to the house so they can renovate those penthouse suites in the hotel, it sure is a strange addiction for the masses. The casino was the perfect place for girls to dress up and flaunt their curves while the guys all tuxedoed-up, going for that high status look to woo them ladies.

Myself on the other hand, I was more into wearing casual gym wear, *yes*, even to the casino. I felt more like myself when I didn't have to worry about matching my shoes to the outfit. However on rare occasions, I'd surrender my comfort zone in order to look dazzling.

So that night, I scavenged through the pile of clothes on my wardrobe floor, and found only slightly creased jeans and a matching white polo shirt, after all there was always the potential I might hook up with someone. To be honest I was a bit too shy to meet new girls but luckily our group was always bringing along new people, which was a nicer way to meet girls through mutual friends in the group.

I clipped on my favourite TAG watch, my friends had all chipped in and given it to me as a birthday present and they knew I wore it everywhere. Soon my friend Tonee arrived to give me a lift to the party. I had met him a few years before as part of a new crew to break away from the past. Sometimes we'd party together or go mountain bike riding or to the gym as we both liked to keep fit. We weren't best mates but he was a great guy that was up to a similar point in his life as me I guess.

It was a nice warm evening and I could see some friends just arriving at the entrance. Tonee chauffeured me right up next to them like a red carpet star and then took off to park the car. Tonee was happy to just have one or two drinks that night and drive us home. Occasionally whenever the designated driver had too many, we'd leave the car in the city or wherever it was and catch a taxi home. We didn't mind paying the $120 parking fine for getting safely back home.

We arrived fairly early, I always liked to get a seat and be comfortable for the night. Get there late and you'd be stuck standing up all night, sucks big time. I was excited to be trying out this club I'd heard about: it had only opened in April that year, we had a private lounge area, alcohol was unlimited and I wasn't driving. Everything was set for a perfect night.

The atmosphere was electric when I walked in. A dark heaving dance floor pierced by coloured strobe lights; smoke machines working their magic and the crowd jumping wildly to Swedish House Mafia's new track, "Don't You Worry Child".

There were plenty of new people and girls to laugh and drink with in our VIP area. I didn't have any great dance moves to bust out but I was having the time of my life as I slammed those shots down: one, two, three. Knocking back whatever came my way as part of the upmarket drinks

CHAPTER 3

package: Hennessy, Martell, Dom Perignon.

I was one of those heavy-drinking, misguided souls who told themselves they could counteract such alcoholic abuse to their bodies with physical redemption and so I told myself I'd go to the gym the next day, pumping iron would help to seep the alcohol back out too.

I was having such a great time that I laughed to myself that my friends would have to tell me tomorrow about all the fun I was having that night, just like they always did. With the music throbbing, I flew wildly into the black void …

∿∿∿

I opened my eyes to a white ceiling. I felt comfortable. I wasn't sure where I was but I felt warm and relaxed. My mum and brother were looking down at me. *That's weird*, I thought. *Okay, I'm in bed, maybe I'm sick?* I still felt very calm. But then I realised my shoes felt uncomfortable. I didn't want them on while I was in bed.

"Can you take off my shoes please?" I asked.

Mum had a strange look on her face. She seemed relieved to hear from me but she looked worried too. She and my brother were sharing strange looks with each other.

HAZARD AHEAD

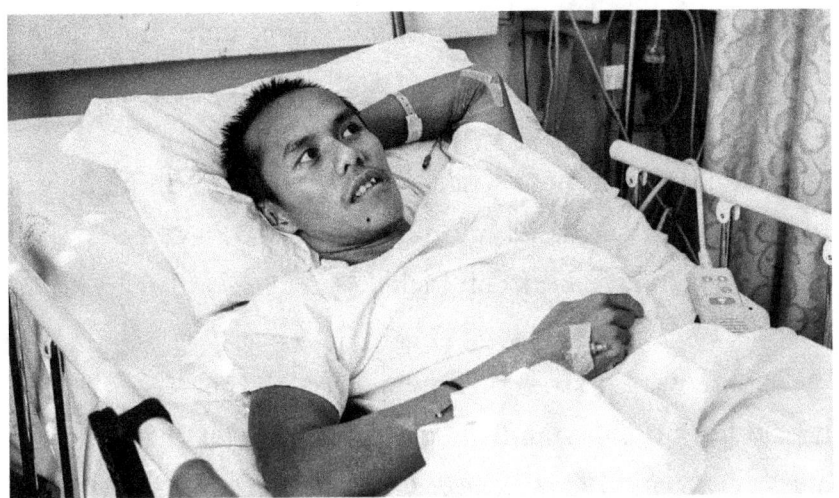

Suspended reality; waking up dazed and confused 18 days after the crash.

"Not right now." Mum replied in a choked voice.

I accepted her answer without question. I didn't ask why. My brother softly explained I'd been in a car accident and was in the hospital. I tried to remember the night before but there was a big black hole. It was much more tempting to drift in and out of sleep for a while.

The next day, I woke up enough to prop myself up in bed slightly. Everything was so orderly and I tried to make sense of my surroundings; the beep of a machine full of cables beside me, a stiff looking curtain, two hard backed chairs, a clipboard hanging off the end of the bed, crisp white sheets tucked in tightly around me.

CHAPTER 3

My eyes followed the line of my thighs under the smooth white sheet ... and how the sheet fell abruptly straight down to the mattress in odd places.

I couldn't compute what I was looking at. Short bulges hid under the sheets where my legs should have been. The lumps looked fake, short and fake. *I'm not looking at my actual body am I?*

There were no toes poking up beneath the sheet: no feet, no ankles, no shins and my right leg ... well that was just entirely *missing. What happened to my legs? Could the doctors be fixing them?*

Hang on a minute; I could *feel* my legs, my calf muscles, and my toes so I didn't really worry. If I could feel them, they must be there somewhere.

"I'm sorry Khoa, they had to amputate your legs to save your life." Mum was in the room again and she finally put words to what I was looking at. *Oh right, I see, okay,* I thought. Those were the facts were they? I had begun to sense I was on medications but even so I thought I was able to accept Mum's words and the evidence before me. I would figure it all out soon.

I also thought I had a recent memory of leaving the hospital and dashing home in a taxi and then coming back again. I assumed I must have done that without legs so I'd be right, I wouldn't dwell on it. I felt a bit detached but thought I understood. *It's okay*, I thought, *it'll all work out*, as I sank back down into oblivion once more.

∼∼∼

Next time I woke I realised I was in the ICU. The nurses kept asking me the same questions over and over every time they saw me. The day, the date, the year, who was the Prime Minister (who can keep up with that anyway?). They kept checking a head injury I had sustained and they were keen to see if I had brain damage.

No wonder Mum was so relieved when I regained consciousness, they hadn't known if I was going to wake up the same person or even wake up at all.

I still had no memory of the accident so over a few days the doctors and my family helped me piece together what had happened. My memory stopped from about 10pm the night of the party in the club. We had to work back and forth to uncover the events.

My friend who I had been living with for about a month had been leaving home around 5am on the morning of Sunday 9th December. He noticed ambulances and police cars attending an accident only a few minutes away from our house.

CHAPTER 3

As he came closer he recognised the car as Tonee's blue Nissan Skyline. He realised there was a good chance that I had probably been in the car as the crash was so close to home. Word quickly spread through the grapevine, that Tonee and I were involved in a serious accident. One of my other friends heard the news and quickly phoned my brother to tell him the injured had been flown to separate hospitals.

Mum was at the grocery shop buying food for a family dinner she had organised for that Sunday night, she liked getting us kids together regularly. She answered a phone call from my brother asking her to meet him at the hospital; he explained that I'd been involved in an accident.

She dropped her shopping and quickly drove with my sister to the Emergency Department of Westmead Hospital. They probably thought, *'What has Khoa done now? We were supposed to be having our family dinner tonight!'*

When my brother arrived, he asked the reception desk if a "Khoa Nam Tran" had been brought in, the woman replied that no, no one had been admitted by that name. Then a passing doctor heard their conversation and said, "We did receive an unidentified male who was airlifted to the hospital this morning. He had no ID but we have his possessions."

My brother went with the doctor who showed him the possessions: *my* possessions. My brother quickly identified my TAG watch. As they reached the E.D, Mum and my sister saw my brother come out of a doorway. His face said it all. It wasn't just a bung up car accident as they assumed but something much more serious. Mum broke down in tears with my sister putting on a brave face to support her.

Looking back at this now, it's hard to imagine anyone coming out of this wreck alive: the positive side to not remembering that fateful night.

Tonee's car was a small two door and I had been sitting in the back when Tonee lost control and hit a power pole at high speed. I don't know how I squished into such a cramped space;

CHAPTER 3

my legs were crushed under the passenger's seat on impact.

My lower left leg was damaged beyond repair and when I arrived in the Emergency Department the doctors put me into an induced coma in order to immediately amputate below the knee. The next problem was my other leg.

My injuries were far from straightforward. My right foot had started to turn black. It was bleeding profusely and not directing enough flow to the muscles. The doctors amputated the foot first, hoping they could get it under control. However the prolific blood loss continued and my leg muscles were deteriorating due to the lack of oxygen and blood so they had to amputate again slightly higher.

I made the doctors work hard that day because this still didn't work. Unstoppable blood loss from that second attempt meant they had to try higher up and amputated just below the knee. Frustrated, the doctors still couldn't get it under control and finally they were forced to amputate above my right knee a few hours after the accident.

Then came the real problem.

"What! It got worse?"

Surely yes, because I was still losing blood to the point where I had received the equivalent blood bank of four adults and it hadn't helped, my leg just kept bleeding out. There was only one last chance for me to survive. However Mum would have to approve the risky procedure first.

The doctor explained to my family that everything they had tried was not working. They had reached the last resort; administering a drug that would effectively clot the blood which was their number one priority. But the caveat was this didn't promise to save me.

On the contrary, the adverse side effects could be damaging and deadly. A heart attack was possible during the administration; I may suffer brain damage, or not survive at all. If Mum went with option one, and said no, then I wouldn't be here. Mum knew there was no choice but to go ahead, anything to save her son.

The medical team saved me.

※

My family and friends sat by my side as I lay in a coma for 18 long days, eventually waking on Boxing Day, December 26 2012. I spent the strangest week in ICU. My friends all came in to see me, which meant so much to me. I thanked them over and over again. To the point they asked me to stop thanking them. I asked them how school was; I thought I was still in high school!

Next I thought I was in a hospital in Panama. When my

CHAPTER 3

friends and family visited I was so amazed and told them, "Thank you for coming to see me! You flew all the way over here for me?" They looked at me strangely and would have thought, *As if! You're not that special!* Ha ha!

I was plagued by thoughts of Tonee. At one point I thought one of my mates who came to visit me actually *was* Tonee. I remember saying to everyone in the room that his alter ego was Tonee, "That's his other name," I said. It was very strange because I didn't accuse him of the accident or anything; I was just so sure that this person was Tonee, walking around like nothing had happened.

I now realise I may have left an indelible scar on my friend who only came to check on my wellbeing, not to be accused of being someone he was not. *Oops, so sorry Cam if you're reading this, it was the drugs I swear!*

Finally I said to the doctor, "Look, I'll just go home for a bit and then catch a taxi back, I promise I'll come back."

"Ah, you can't do that, you can't walk."

Yeah right, I thought, *what would you know! You say I can't walk but I will.*

Besides I was sure I could still feel the nerves in my legs and even the tightening of my calf muscle. I was adamant I'd done it once already without legs. I hadn't had any hassles before when I had nicked home because I wanted to use my own bathroom.

So I said to him, "Remember I came back that other time didn't I?"

I know what you're thinking, don't worry; my fantasyland came crashing down that night while still in ICU. *That's it*, I had thought, *I need to use the toilet and I'm getting off this bed.*

It didn't register that I still had the catheter tubes in. The side of the bed was lowered and I shuffled over and launched off. The bed was raised quite high and *man*, I fell like Humpty Dumpty!

It was a bloody hard fall. I lay there stunned for a few seconds, struggling to realise what had happened, looking at my legs laying awkwardly and shorter than I expected them to be. The nurses came running over, "What are you doing?" They cried.

"I wanted to use the bathroom," I replied.

"But you can't!" They shook their heads.

"I think I know that now," I whispered slowly in reply.

And that my friends, was my light bulb moment; I really did lose my legs.

The painkillers had eased off; my mind was clear. I wanted to wake up from this dream, this nightmare *now*! I wanted to go back! Go back! Go back! Change things! I did not want to accept this reality.

As they lifted me back onto bed, desperate questions crowded my mind. *How will I walk again? How will I drive*

CHAPTER 3

again? How will I live again?

I thought of all the things I couldn't do; walk, run, ride, drive, jetski and who knew what else. The emotion I felt overwhelmed me; an intense low deep throbbing in my ears that wouldn't stop. The realisation of what I had lost felt enormous. I thought the most fundamental thing a human needed was a leg to stand on.

The world around me started to shrink. I felt useless. *Who would love me?* A black vortex was sucking all my independence away, slowly diminishing me through a tide of hopelessness. I thought people would judge me as a cripple and I would be thrown out of the circle of norms. *Fucking fuck! What was I going to do? How would I get through this?* I felt empty, defeated … lifeless.

ᴎᴜᴜᴜ

I was also facing a challenge of a different kind when I found out the full consequences of the accident. Tonee had received horrendous head injuries and suspected brain damage. He was being treated in a different hospital that specialised in brain trauma.

There had also been someone in the front passenger

seat who unfortunately felt the full impact of the collision. A young woman I didn't know very well, Becca, only 18, had been at the party and somehow, I can't remember why, she was in the car too. Becca had died at the scene.

Finding out about Tonee and Becca was harder to accept than losing my legs. What a horrendous price to pay for a night out! *What had happened? What went wrong?* I just didn't know. I did not believe Tonee would have been drunk, we all knew the deal when it was your turn to drive, and I'd driven and stayed sober plenty of times too. *Was it speed perhaps?*

For the first time, I considered how drunk I had been and whether alcohol played a part in me being in this situation. I couldn't remember a thing. *How was I going to help anyone figure out what happened? To give people some answers? Why did I get so drunk? Why did I always get so drunk? Was it to have fun? Didn't I have heaps of fun anyway without getting drunk?* Clouds of questions swirled around my head, swamping me.

I was still hooked up to painkillers and the doctor said I could press the button any time I was feeling pain. Technically I wasn't feeling much pain but I thought, *why not?* I might press that damn button anyway; maybe I'd become a drug addict. *Who cares?*

I tried it for a few nights; it had a lockout of five-minute intervals preventing me from constantly taking the drug but I made sure that when those five minutes were up, I pressed that button straight away to keep the emotions at bay. It also kept me awake throughout those nights; I listened to the beep of the heart monitor for hours on end and ironically this sound reminded me how precious every moment in life was.

Time slowed down for me in this quiet, heavy period of realisation. For a while I tried out the mentality of 'what-ifs' and 'should haves' and I wallowed in a daze of self-pity. I reached over to press the button once more but this time I heard a little voice say — *shit Khoa, this could be bad buddy. You should stop.* That same little voice had more to say — *life's not going to wait for you Man!*

What happens when you fall deep into a dark hole? It might take a while but you climb out of it! A question burst in my mind loud and clear.

Why should I prevent myself from still living life to the fullest?

I could see the dead end road ahead of me if I let negative defeatist thoughts take hold. I felt there must be another way of looking at my situation and I wondered what possibilities might come in my new form. After all, life is still one amazing ride, I held onto that thought.

My family came in every day to support (and feed) me.

CHAPTER 3

Despite what had happened I didn't want to be seen as a victim of a car crash. I remembered the bubbly guy I was and didn't want to let the accident redefine me into a sad case. Slowly, through this process I realised I could simply *refuse* to let the accident define who I was.

Instead this whole crazy journey was beginning to crystallise the value of who I really was underneath everything. And it became clear to me that I still had great power in the choices I was about to make.

I look back and thank my inner humour that I'd been born with and always relied on to enjoy life. I thought about the brighter side of being legless; my feet won't stink, shoe size won't be an issue, I won't get cold feet, I won't care if I wear shorts on a cold, windy day. I'd literally have legs of steel. I smiled my first proper smile since waking up.

I was starting to create a vision of how to live my best life. I loved fun and laughter and that was a virtue I could still enjoy and use as a tool to climb out of this hole. I remember a wonderful nurse Hellen, whose special kindness really helped me through this time. Her compassion seemed to give me strength; it was such a simple beautiful gift she gave me whenever she came to see me. Her warmth, her smile, the extra time she took to really talk to me to see how I was going and if I needed anything. She was also really positive, like she believed in my recovery without question and that I could still do great things. I wanted to think like that too.

I moved out of ICU into a ward. I was still wearing a hospital gown with the easy access opening at the back. I couldn't resist having some fun and flashed my friends when they came to visit. They not only got to see my private parts, but also a tube stuck up my exit point, I probably scarred them for life but hey, it was hilarious and made them realise Khoa was back!

I wasn't magically, suddenly, permanently happy about losing my legs, but I didn't want to waste time with regret, so every time I stumbled into that rabbit hole of negative thoughts, I'd talk myself out of it, "*Khoa, you just survived a horrific accident, you are a bloody trooper for beating the odds! Khoa, look forward to what you will achieve in the future, set your goals and don't let anything stop you from achieving it. After all, you are still breathing. Let's move on!*"

I told myself, "*No looking back, get cracking!*" I did not want to be held back by the past while life inevitably moved on.

So I accepted what happened.

Pretty quickly you might say, but that's the point. Imagine if I took a year or longer to accept my situation, a whole year out of my life wasted to sadness, hopelessness or regret. No way! For me, it took a few days to climb out of that hole, but once I decided to, I started climbing fast. I felt what happened, had happened for a reason and this was the beginning of the new Khoa.

CHAPTER 3

I kept on climbing, I didn't just want to get back to being old Khoa, I wanted to stand as tall as my inner self was telling me to. To really explore what I was made of and how that would look in my life.

Standing tall has become a natural mindset for me, pulling me ever upward to persevere through what could have been a one-way path of agony and self-pity. Standing tall has lifted me away from having a victim mindset that surely my caring peers would have not questioned because of the visual impact of my injury. But I knew I could rise above all the preconceived ideas of my condition and circumstances.

I asked myself what I was grateful for and the answers kept coming. I still had my sense of humour and spirit, I had plenty of movement and would be able to get around in a wheelchair, I had a good chance of walking with the aid of prosthetics in the future, and I could even get taller.

Yes - I would be able to raise or lower my height as I pleased. Who says we shrink when we age? And I can actually say I'm legless even before the drinks come around.

One decision was clear, no more alcohol. I knew that part of my life was over with no regrets; I wanted to take full control on how I chose to live my life going forward.

CHAPTER 4
ROLLERCOASTER TO RECOVERY

I was transforming day by day. From the gloom of defeat, I started to notice every good thing that happened like a spark of hope. I was so grateful for everything, still feeling amazed that so many people took time out of their lives to come and see me.

Even people I hadn't seen since high school. The time

CHAPTER 4

with those old mates was great. Within minutes we'd be laughing and teasing each other and they could tell it was still me, they saw passed the amputation and that it hadn't changed me.

When the medication wore off about ten days after I woke up, I was still quite sore from the whiplash and bruising from the seatbelt, but thank God I was wearing one. The hefty scar I have across my chest highlights how these simple devices really do save lives.

Being bed bound for weeks, I didn't have the luxury of getting myself to the bathroom to shower and wash. It was something I really missed. Bath time was simply a bucket of warm water and small cotton towels. I stayed in bed trying to clean wherever I could reach and then the nurse would help me with my flipside; not half as satisfying as that burst of steam and heat from a toasty shower. I wondered if I'd ever get to experience that again.

The medication also killed my taste buds for a while which was a bummer. I ate mainly watermelon and mango at first and then Mum started bringing in home cooked meals to help tempt me and put on some weight.

You don't realise how glancing in the mirror regularly keeps you in perspective. When I could finally use the commode wheelchair to take myself to the bathroom, brushing my teeth was my first call to action. As I gazed at my reflection over

My mum. My rock.

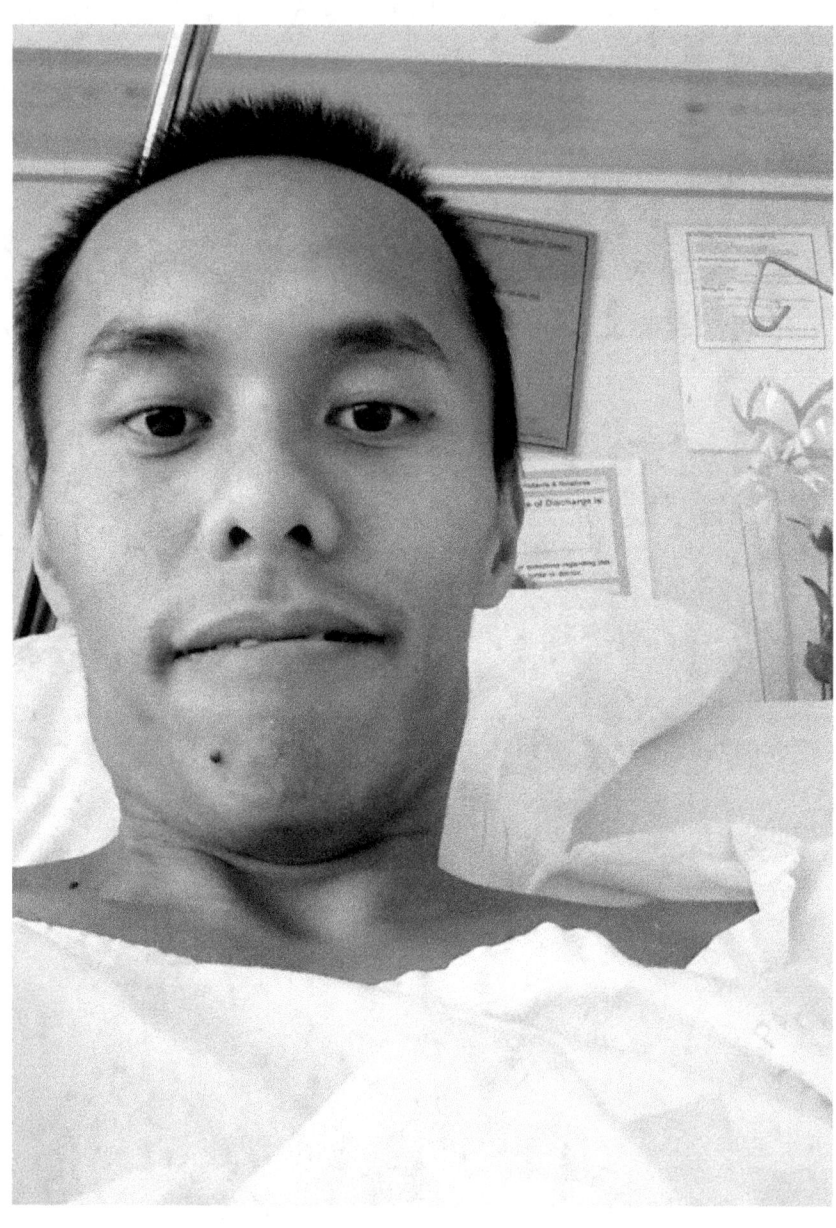

I lost more than I had thought.

the sink I was shocked, my face was so skinny; I could see my cheekbones! I honestly had thought I was physically still the same Khoa, just without legs, but I didn't realise what many surgeries and an induced coma would do to a person, *Pffft*, so naive of me. I actually lost 25 kgs and got down to only 45kgs.

Anyhow, back to the food, I was on a roll when I could taste again, how could I settle for hospital food when there was crispy chicken and Bánh xèo (Vietnamese pancake) to devour? Mum's family dinners became the best take-away family feasts delivered right to my hospital room. I also welcomed any fast food donations my friends brought in to fatten me up again. Those chicken McNuggets surely did rejuvenate my taste buds after being waylaid for so long.

ᴨᴜᴜ

I needed numerous procedures in the two months I was in hospital. My legs were still open wounds for a while and I needed a vac pack sealed to my stumps to drain away the fluid. Gradually through a series of skin graft procedures, my legs started to heal over.

I was a regular to surgery and I would always joke with the orderlies as they wheeled me along to theatre. I was surprised

CHAPTER 4

that one remembered me years later when I visited hospital for an appointment. He said, "Hey, I remember you, you're that guy who smiled and laughed on the way to theatre!" See? I'm unforgettable, ha ha!

The surgeons took skin from my thighs to close the wounds, so I have a ton of scars all over my legs. The most painful experience was when it came time to remove the sticky black gauze material over the new skin. I have a fairly high pain threshold but **OMG**! Peeling it off was absolute agony! I screamed and swore. I had to psyche myself up to it each time and then I would suck madly on the green whistle for pain relief but nothing could dull that sort of pain, it was a totally new experience for me, not something I ever wish to repeat.

I was learning a little bit more about the accident. Apparently there weren't any skid marks before the bend near the power pole so speed was a likely factor. It looked like the car had clipped the curb, jumped onto the nature strip and hit the pole on the passenger's side.

It had to be investigated as part of the eligibility process for me to qualify for Lifetime Care, the government support scheme that pays for treatment, rehabilitation and care for people who have been severely injured in a motor accident in New South Wales.[2]

I was grateful for that too. Imagine if the accident had happened in one of the developing countries I had visited,

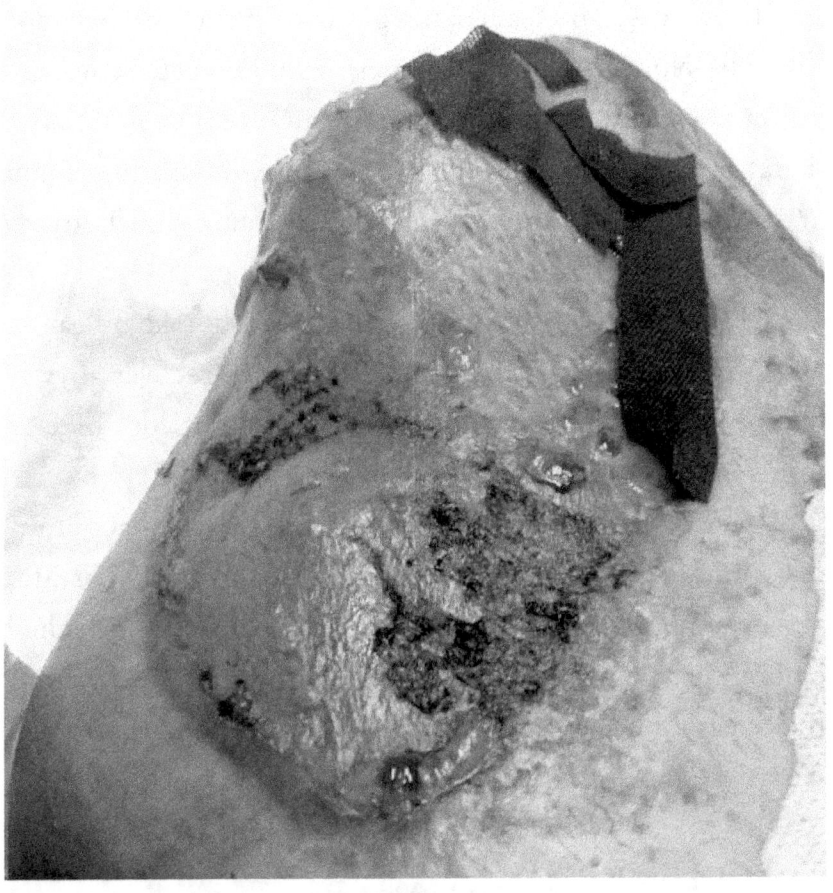

*Just an ordinary day peeling off the gauze—f#*k!*

it would have been an even tougher journey with enormous financial stress. My friend Tonee is also cared for by the Lifetime Care program and this provides him with 24-hour care in the right care facility without the financial stress.

CHAPTER 4

There was also a legal battle going on trying to determine the facts behind the accident, as these would affect the compensation payout from the third party insurance. I couldn't offer much except my memories leading up to 10pm that night and that Tonee was the designated driver and as such, to my knowledge Tonee had not been drink driving.

I knew any compensation could possibly take a year or more to come through but I needed time to recover anyway before thinking about what my future might look like in terms of employment.

After being bedbound for weeks, I was excited about my first time in a wheelchair. I could cruise down the corridor and explore on my own, it gave me a sense of freedom again. I embraced my new wheels and wanted to modify them, upgrade the specs! Unfortunately Lifetime Care didn't approve it. They have no appreciation for good-looking wheels.

∩∪∩∪

After two months in Westmead hospital, I was moved to a rehabilitation hospital in Fairfield. Different specialists came to see me and assess my situation, my options going forward and to help me with a recovery program.

I was keen to start rehabilitation and especially to get back into fitness. It felt different than before the accident when I had exercised as a way to balance out a night of heavy drinking. Now every movement had a purpose; the small goal was to be stronger than the day before and the bigger goal was to start living my new life and find out how much I could do with my new body.

I pushed myself more than I was supposed to in order to test my limits and then break through them. Every day I'd do light weight training, leg raises and band work to strengthen my core and limbs. I wanted my legs to be as strong as possible for when I met my prosthetist.

I consider myself one of the lucky ones because I don't get phantom pains anymore from where my legs used to be. For a few weeks after the coma, I did feel like my legs and feet were still there and I would feel sharp jolts of pain at the end of my stumps that kept me awake many nights.

Gradually, thankfully, those pains disappeared. My personal perspective is that my mind now computes exactly where my legs end because it was not elective surgery that put me here but life-saving surgery. Some people with diabetes medically 'elect' to have a limb removed yet they experience phantom feelings and pains for many years afterwards.

I have a clear separation between my last memory of standing on two feet and then waking up without legs and

CHAPTER 4

learning what had to happen to save my life. I am grateful I've had a relatively pain free journey so far.

The rehab centre kept me busy each day; I didn't have much time on my own between training, visitors and specialists. Any time I felt bored I had my gadgets; at the time it was the latest Samsung Galaxy Note 2 to play with and car magazines to focus on. At that point I didn't think about whether I'd ever be able to drive again, I knew it was a day-by-day journey and that driving was a dream for another day, a far off dream to be honest.

I still had an artsy eye so I wouldn't just read about the cars in the magazine. I would also appreciate the photographers' work in nailing those amazing shots. You know that kid who cuts pictures out of magazines to stick on their wall? Yup, that was me, although it was cars not bikini models … okay, maybe a few models, but I had way more car pictures plastered over them.

∿∿∿

The day finally arrived when I met Stefan Laux, my prosthetist. He was a smart, serious but friendly guy who not only went to great lengths to figure out my best options, he laughed at my lame jokes too. Stefan genuinely wanted to help me and I could tell he loved his job. He explained all the details of the prosthetic sockets that would be cast to fit my stumps and that prosthetic legs are then attached to the sockets.

Before you become an amputee, you cannot know what you would endure, in terms of fitting new legs. Due to my love of technology I was actually excited that I could have carbon fibre sockets and legs that would make me look half-man half-robot.

Stefan did mention the idea of osseointegration where a titanium rod is implanted into your living bone, but at the time I thought sockets were the best option in line with my techno expectations.

You could say I didn't really know what I needed. I was fixated by one particular model of legs because I liked the thought of having an edge over the other guys trying to impress the ladies; I was thinking *Iron Man* appeal.

When I told Stefan which legs I really wanted, he looked at me like I was a lost puppy, "Khoa, there's a model that's even better than that, I was planning to suggest those to Lifetime Care to approve, because you're still young and very active, you will need the best of the best."

I was ecstatic; awesome legs had just become more awesome! A five-day battery life compared to two, they

CHAPTER 4

needed charging just like your phone. Plus with these I could run up to 15km/hour. Okay, maybe I never actually liked running and I probably wouldn't use that particular feature but it was good to know that I had all the bells and whistles. I was seriously becoming the next AI.

That's how I imagined it, a world of cyborgs and I was one of the pioneering test dummies. I was thankful that the robotic-looking legs that Stefan suggested were approved and I couldn't wait to show off my new bling. I was very fortunate in having them approved; some people weren't so lucky if they didn't meet certain conditions.

I remember how Stefan really went in to bat for his patients. He was passionate when he explained to me that you can't put a price on someone's leg and the cheaper mechanical ones would not allow me the full benefit of wearing sockets. His point of view really opened my eyes on how to stand your ground and fight for the best option for yourself as an amputee who deserves every chance to regain as much movement and opportunity as possible.

For the insurers though, they did put a price on them, and they wanted to minimise that price. There were many hoops to jump through at each step. They wouldn't want to give everyone a top end leg, as not everyone would be suited or make full use of it.

There are a lot of different features in a $20,000 leg

compared to a $100,000 leg but generally speaking, the safety features, such as locking out the knee to prevent falls or adapting to different terrains, are more prevalent in a high-end leg. Thanks to Stefan's support I realised I deserved this advanced mobile technology as much as anybody did.

༄

Over a few weeks, my left socket was the first to be cast and fitted below the knee fairly easily. I remember the moment clearly when I braced my arms firmly against the parallel bars to finally stand up. It was exhilarating. To feel my muscles redistribute my weight to accommodate a vertical position was so satisfying. And I could look my physios in the eye from an equal height, not propped up in bed.

Honestly, the only time my bottom had been free from the bed mattress was the occasional time I turned over to my stomach to relieve my backpressure. This is a common practice for patients constantly lying in bed recommended by the physios.

Now that I was actually standing with one leg, a huge smirk spread across my face. Even the concentration to stay upright was thrilling and I wanted to leap for joy! Luckily I

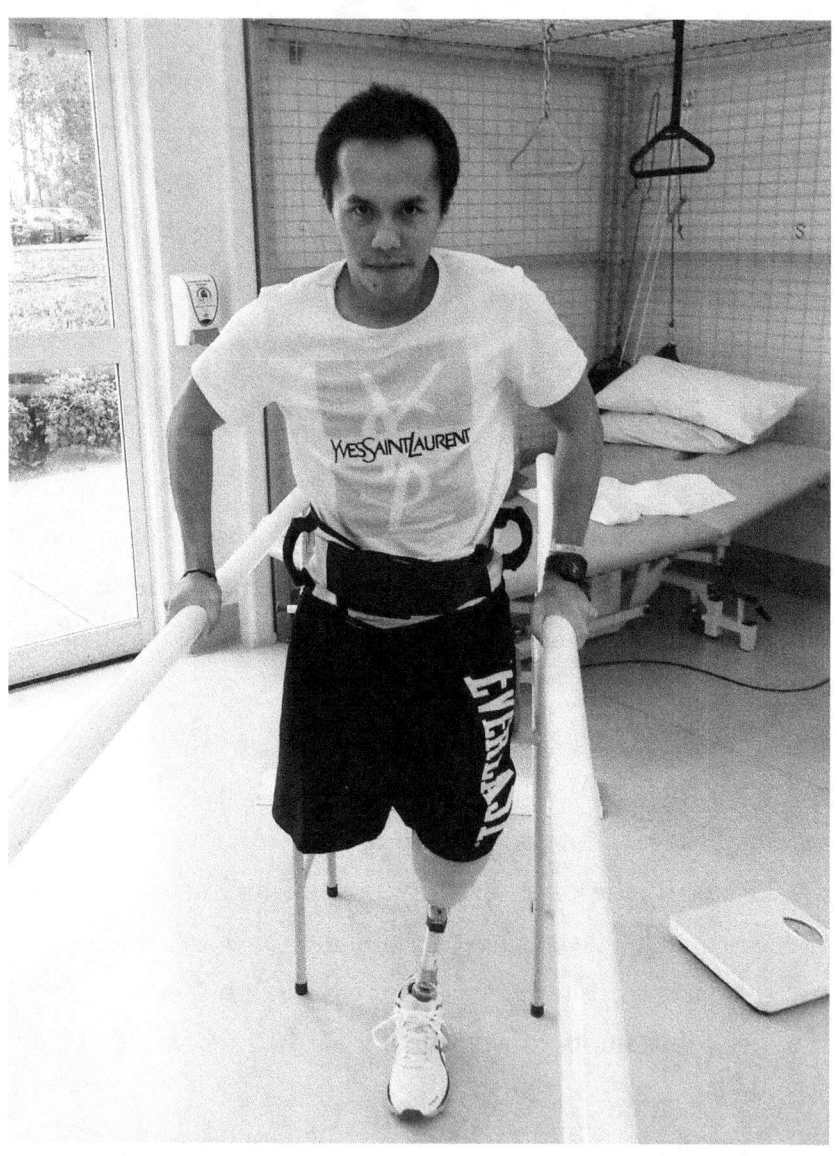

The very first time my arse was unsupported and I was vertical! February 2013 at Fairfield Rehab hospital.

resisted the temptation, which would have been fun but also create more setbacks.

The right cast was more difficult as it had to cover my stump right up to my hip. There were quite a few trial and errors with that one and it ended up so much bigger than I anticipated but I was just eager to get cracking. A week after I tried my left socket leg, I was finally standing on my two socket legs. It was bloody hard work but I did it!

As wonderful as that feeling was, questions and doubts soon crept in as I began to realise how difficult the sockets were to put on; much more difficult than putting on socks.

It could take ten minutes or longer to attach them and a little voice inside asked, *Will it really take me this long just to get out of bed every single day? Will I look forward to taking off the prosthetics at the end of the day like taking off shoes after a hard day's work? I thought I'd want them on every second. What happens if I need to go to the bathroom urgently while legless, literally?* Argh no - that would not be a great outcome for anyone I thought as my hopes fell.

I compared it to that deflated feeling you get after buying a car without test-driving it and ending up with a lemon; your hopes are dashed and you think how naïve you were.

In my case though I didn't have the luxury of picking and choosing new sockets. The fact was my high level of scarring meant the sockets were just not comfortable because there

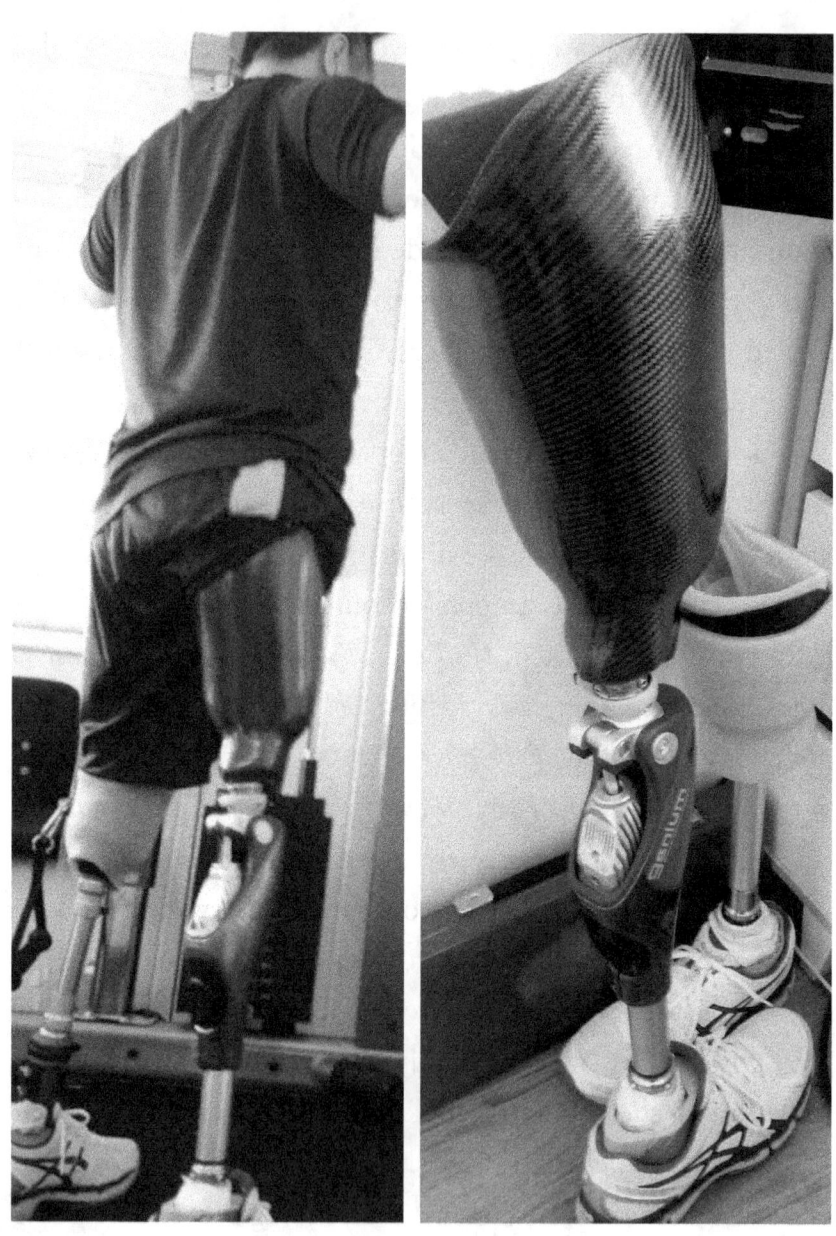

The sockets were big and bulky but I was determined to make them work.

wasn't much 'meat' left on my stumps to cushion the contact between skin and socket. I assumed this discomfort must be the life of an amputee now; I would just have to adjust to it and make the most out of it.

Assuming it would all get easier with practice I remained optimistic and enjoyed my 30th birthday while in rehab. My family were acting a little strange that day saying, "We got you a cake, why don't we go somewhere else to eat it? The common room?"

So I wheeled myself out towards the communal kitchen area and was amazed to see a big group of my friends there to surprise me. I usually have a pretty good radar for that type of thing and have had to act surprised a few times in the past but that day, I was overwhelmed to be genuinely taken by surprise at their thoughtfulness. I'm not a teary guy but I felt so appreciative to see all my friends come in to see me on my birthday. Another moment to be grateful for and it gave me a well-timed boost.

After months of being looked after by many wonderful doctors, nurses, physiotherapists and orderlies, the moment

CHAPTER 4

finally arrived to leave the hospital and return home to my new life; to take the next step towards my independence. I knew I'd have to rely on my family for many things but I was at least strong enough to move myself around to a point, like swinging myself into the front seat of the car, I didn't need to be carried.

The occupational therapist recommended some modifications at home so we adapted a few areas for me to move around safely. Safety rails were installed in the bathroom and

My surprise 30th birthday at the rehab hospital really gave me a boost.

a ramp to get to the back door. The front door had steps so it made more sense to access the house through the back door via the driveway.

Remember how I loved using our steep driveway as a downhill ramp to reach insane speeds on my pushbike? Well now it felt like a death trap with its 45-degree angle. It was a mission for all of us (Mum, bro and me) to push me up the driveway in my new wheels. It was even harder to bring me downhill as the momentum was against us.

I quickly got over any idea to try to do it myself. Mum would park the family car in front of the driveway to act as my buffer from rolling onto the road, but the angle was so steep that rolling onto the road would have been the least of my worries!

It was a pretty strange feeling coming back to my childhood home after a life changing three months. Mum gave up her sewing job to be my carer until I could become more mobile on my own. I was determined to walk and be independent again but didn't know how long such a feat would actually take. My brother helped me a lot too and a nurse would pop in to deliver supplies of dressings and bandages that I had learned to change myself.

Home was my safe place with only family around who understood and supported me. I was still feeling positive but it felt different in the real world as I started to come into

CHAPTER 4

contact with a wider circle of people; different friends or their kids or people from my wider circle that I hadn't seen yet. My first trip into the outside world was a shock. Mum and my brother took me to the local Cabramatta shops wheeling me in my wheelchair.

There were so many eyes looking at me; young and old, it seemed like everyone was staring and thinking, *That guy's got no legs!* I was so skinny too; I guess I wasn't looking at the top of my game. I tried to put on a brave face but it clouded me inside.

In April 2013, after being home for a few weeks, I was surprised that my right stump was still weeping through the bandages and they needed to be changed so often. Every night I wrapped a large type of 'nappy' around my stump because it would bleed so much at night. The doctors in hospital had said it was normal and that the hole would close up.

I went to a check-up appointment with one of the doctors who performed my surgery. When I mentioned the oozing he decided to take an x-ray, while keeping the padding and bandages on. He held the x-ray up to the light and he said everything looked okay.

I was looking at the x-ray too, "What's that squiggly line?" I asked. Lucky I did.

The doctor looked closer and thought it might just be the bandage. He suggested taking another x-ray without the bandage on.

Sure enough though, the squiggly line was still there. "Ah," said the doctor, "You have to go back to hospital."

The doctor explained some of the gauze packing in the wound must have been accidently left in when they stitched me up in surgery. Since then my body had been rejecting the foreign object that had been left in my right leg. It was actually lucky that my body had an outlet for the weeping, which is the body's way of saying, "Get out!" The alternative was to keep all the ooze inside and fester into God knows what.

The surgical assistants are supposed to count the gauze that goes in and then count it back out again. I guess I need to thank the tiny bit of radiation they put in the gauze so it showed up on the x-ray, which is precisely why it was designed that way so it must have happened before to other poor buggers.

I was philosophical about returning to hospital for another month. However it did mean more surgery and more scarring. I was still feeling self-conscious about the amount of scarring I had on my legs. I wore protective

CHAPTER 4

sleeves over my legs for months after the surgery. Yes, they were for protection from bumps and falls but I was still worried about how it looked. I deliberately chose to wear long shorts to hang over my legs as well.

Over time I learned to embrace every part of myself and how the scars represent my story, that they are actually something to be proud of as who I am and what I have overcome along the way.

Even though I had accepted what had happened relatively quickly because I didn't want to waste a moment, I realised that to fully accept what happened I needed to fully accept how I looked as well. While it was part of my identity, it didn't define me. I was starting to realise how standing tall and staying positive, can overshadow anything that tries to hold you back.

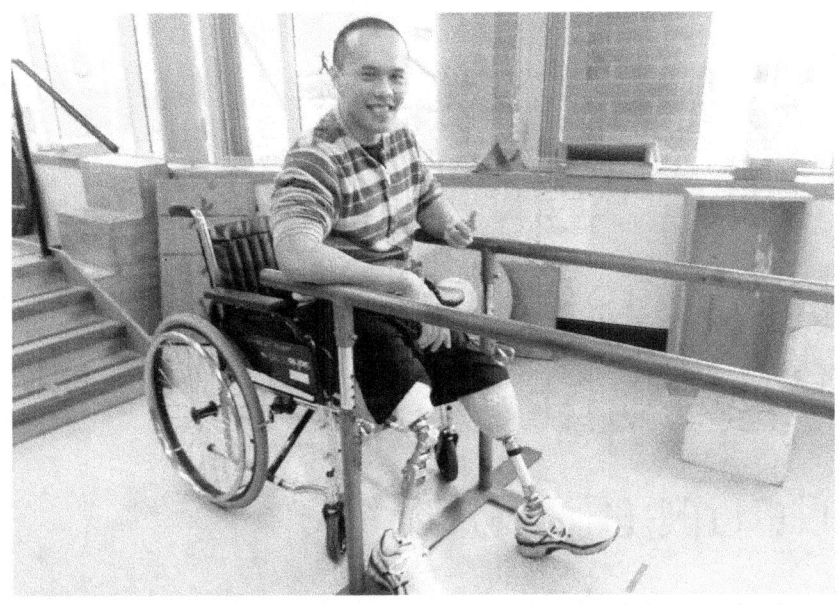

A typical day as an out-patient in rehab, sometimes it was hard to muster up a smile but I stayed focused.

Khoa is sharing more in his INTERACTIVE book.

See exclusive videos, audios and photos.

DOWNLOAD it now at
deanpublishing.com/legless

> Smile through the tough times because you are the light to guide yourself out of the darkness.

CHAPTER 5
THE SLOW LANE

A month later I returned home to begin my recovery again. I was grateful once more for my family who had all made sacrifices for me to get this far. My beautiful grandmother had still been living with Mum after my accident.

When I returned home as a 'patient' with a long road to recovery ahead, my mum was really worried how she could give both of us, my 77-year-old grandmother and me, the care we needed. My grandmother still had a lot of family back

CHAPTER 5

in Vietnam and as she had never learnt to speak English, it could still feel isolating for her here sometimes.

After a lot of thought and discussion, my grandmother decided to return to Vietnam, to join her siblings in the south. We've missed her very much since she left and it was a big change not having her close by.

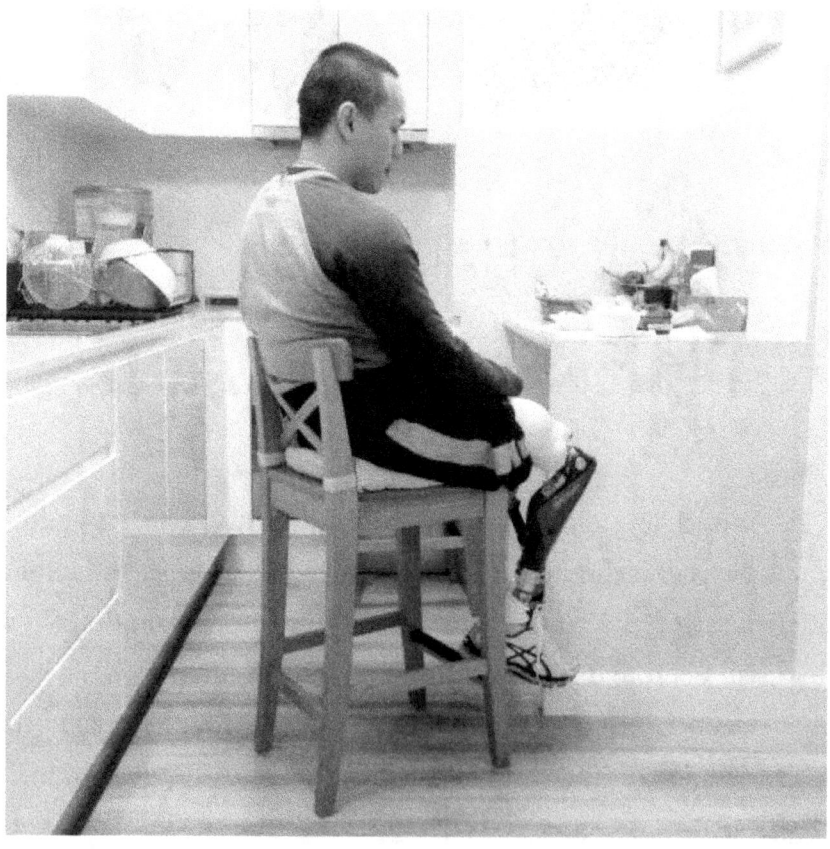

The reality of being an amputee was tough; every task was a mission.

Over the next four months I rarely left the house. Friends would come by to hang out and chat with me, I watched a stack of TV and I had the fast-paced world of the internet at my fingertips to keep me occupied. Nothing beats real life action, but for people in similar situations to me, the internet can be a great tool to connect and feel part of the world.

Although this was the quietest time of my life, it was also the most intense as the mountain of learning to walk again loomed in front of me. Gym wasn't an option yet, so I trained myself at home focusing on regaining my strength (think push-up Olympics) and becoming familiar with my new legs.

Does anyone know the feeling when your trainer at the gym says, "Right - it's leg day today," and everyone groans? Well every day became 'leg day' in my case as I learnt how to walk again. The sheer amount of mental and physical sweat involved was not what I signed up for!

I'll be honest and admit putting my sockets to practical use still wasn't a raging success. They were stiff and awkward and the risk of falling was always on my mind. Constant bruising and skin chafing were more hurdles to bear that I hadn't foreseen.

CHAPTER 5

My dreams of strutting like a celebrity robot quickly evaporated in the face of all these unexpected little niggles that inhibited my chance to walk around comfortably. Just navigating around the house had plenty of challenges, which left me too tired to move by the end of the day.

The speed of my life had reduced down to a snail's pace and my days and weeks became so repetitious I felt dormant, like I was in hibernation. I still had that little spark of eagerness in me to simply get up and start walking but I soon realised the toughest challenge of all was the time it would take to heal.

I was still far from independent, relying fully on my mum or brother to help wheel me to the car, carefully preventing my wheelchair from freewheeling down the driveway. I was conscious when Mum was helping me down the slope as it was a lot of weight for her to manage and she wasn't as strong as my brother.

I didn't let this reality depress me though, I decided to see it as another challenge along the road so I reigned in my long-term expectations and focused step-by-step on what I could achieve in realistic terms. I would try everything possible to give the prosthetic legs their best chance of success.

As well as walking round the house I practised walking in a little laneway nearby. It allowed more space to practise my steps than inside the house and it also represented what the

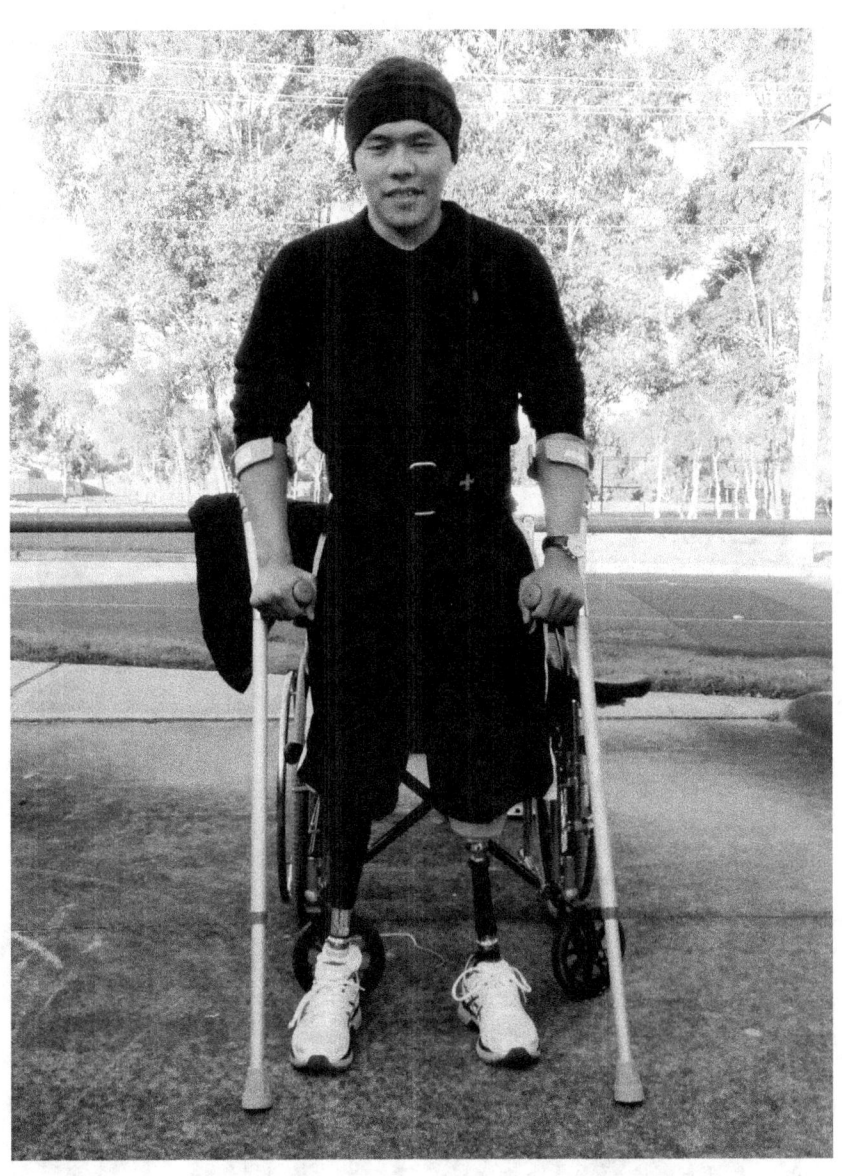

My first taste of the real world away from a controlled environment. I wasn't nervous; I was ecstatic. I was going to improve every time I went out.

CHAPTER 5

real world offered in terms of terrain, you never knew what you'd get.

I would set little goals of trying to walk with only one stick (or crutch) for 20 metres and then after a few days I would try walking the same distance without either stick. It

Sometimes I preferred to just roll around.

was uplifting when I achieved my goal. Walking had become something scary; there was so much to get used to. I'd last about 20 minutes before I'd plonk back down exhausted into the wheelchair.

I was also driven to the rehab centre at Liverpool once a week. This outlet turned out to be really important in my mental recovery. Along with seeing a physio for my rehab session, it also allowed me to regularly connect with other fresh amputees trying to get their life back on track. It was so good to realise that I wasn't alone in this and I met people from all walks of life who were going through their own journeys at similar stages with similar challenges.

One patient I met explained their amputation was a result of diabetes. Another suffered a motocross accident with an above knee amputation. There were so many stories as to why they lost a limb, and I had mine.

You could say this was my very own support group and each week we would see each other's achievements and chit chat about life and how we were coping. The group helped me feel connected and supported and encouraged me to keep aiming for little achievements I could brag about the following week.

CHAPTER 5

In the middle of the year, I was taken by surprise when my skin started to break out in acne, which I'd never really suffered from before. I thought it was normal at first and assumed it would clear up. I tried the usual steps but watched on helplessly as it kept getting worse.

Sexy Khoa! 18 months of stubborn cystic acne until I found the right treatment.

They weren't those common little five-day pimples, these became large looking welts on my face from the blocked pores and infected area going deep into my skin. It really didn't help how I was feeling in terms of my looks. I'm not obsessed with how people look but by then I felt people were staring at my legless state *and* my acne.

Eventually I was diagnosed with cystic acne, the most severe form of acne. It was hard to pinpoint why I was getting it as an adult. Perhaps hormone imbalances to do with internal changes my body had experienced. There's no definitive answer. It went on for about a year and a half. Antibiotics didn't work so I needed some pretty killer medication to finally reduce the outbreaks.

Managing this condition along with learning to walk again, was a really hard period but I never let myself stop and dwell too much or ask why me. I accepted what was and when something didn't pan out, I was already planning the next option to try. I would leave no stone unturned to find a way forward.

As you can probably guess, I still wasn't loving my sockets. Aside from the time they took to get on and their general discomfort, there was also the risk of developing skin breakages over the stump caused by the sockets themselves. The skin was just so thin, too thin to take the pressure of pressing onto the socket. It's a bit like the skin on your knuckle when you make a fist.

CHAPTER 5

In August I did get a skin breakdown and I waited impatiently for three weeks in my wheelchair while it healed. I hadn't knocked my stump on anything; it was simply from wearing the socket so I was frustrated that there was this constant risk of setback caused by the very device that was designed to help me.

∿∿∿

I must have been managing okay though, because Mum suggested going to Vietnam in October 2013, ten months after the accident. At first I was surprised that she thought that was an option for me but she was so eager to see Grandma and other relatives, that when my brother and his girlfriend added their support, I became really excited about getting out of the house on an adventure.

I decided not to take my sockets; I just couldn't manoeuvre well enough in them. I was still worried about the risk of skin breakages so far from my doctors, so I packed plenty of saline solution to bath any wounds that might develop.

I had plenty of questions and concerns, not only was it my first trip to Vietnam but it was also my first crack at travelling in a wheelchair. I had thought Vietnam was a third world

Dining at the famous Lunch Lady in Ho Chi Minh City: made so popular by the American celebrity chef, the late Anthony Bourdain.

Mum was excited to show us where she grew up and see Grandma again.

country (it's not by the way, think fast moving developing nation) and wondered what it would be like for wheelchairs: *How would I cross the road? What accessibility to toilets and showers was there?*

In the end there was nothing to worry about. Besides a forklift that had to lift me down from the plane onto the tarmac once we arrived, everything went smoothly. My mum, brother and his girlfriend supported me everywhere. Mum actually wouldn't let me out of her sight when we were away from the hotel. I spent an adventurous two weeks there meeting family for the first time.

My brother had been to Vietnam before but I was uncovering a part of myself that I'd never given much attention to. I didn't know much about my relatives over in the motherland. It was occasionally discussed when Mum would ring Grandma and see how she was. I was curious to know more but I knew Mum had a bunch of mixed up emotions from her earlier life so I had never pushed her to tell me all about her homeland and family.

When I finally met my relatives, they were so caring and happy to have finally met me. Mum had talked about me a lot over the phone, kind of gloating that I was a trooper for going through all the hardships associated with being a car crash survivor. They saw past my wheelchair and made me feel comfortable from the get-go. Meeting up with Grandma

CHAPTER 5

again was especially exciting, she was really content and was amazed at how well I looked compared to when she had left Sydney.

I'm very fortunate to live in Australia as we have one of the best healthcare systems in the world. I can't fathom what people with a disability in Vietnam have to go through to get decent support.

I remember visiting the main market areas of Ho Chi Minh City. On the footpath, I often saw a guy who had both legs amputated above the knee. He was making ends meet by begging for money. He didn't have prosthetic legs, as that would be a luxury out of reach to most citizens. Instead, he was using two steel bowls to shuffle around on the ground. Like the saying goes, "Where there's a will, there's a way."

The trip was amazing even though it wasn't how I assumed I'd see my parents' homeland for the first time. I wasn't able to go sightseeing at that point but I knew it was a huge achievement regardless. Not something I had imagined I could do even a few months previously.

There was one imperfect moment when we landed back in Sydney on Vietnam Airlines. They should have had an aisle wheelchair available for me to move from the plane seat back to my own wheelchair situated down the boarding tunnel. For whatever reason, it wasn't there.

After some fruitless and time consuming discussions, a

sturdy looking flight attendant offered to piggyback me down the aisle back to my own chair. To this day I'm not sure if he was joking or not but I didn't care, I just needed a ride to that boarding tunnel. I wasn't that heavy at the time: 67kg of pure fat and a little bit of muscle.

I could have kicked up a fuss and demanded *A Current Affair* turn up immediately, but I'm not a big complainer and prefer the easiest most practical option available. So I replied, "Come on then, you can drag me out if you want to, just get me out."

Everyone was a bit surprised but I see each moment as a challenge to make people smile while getting the job done, so it was mission accomplished on both counts that day.

∿∿

My sockets were waiting patiently for me on my return. I admit I struggled to find the motivation to wear them again as I continued with rehab. I thought about how long I had been trying to make them work and how awkward and detached from me they felt. That's when a little memory surfaced in my mind from one of my earliest conversations with Stefan.

Stefan had mentioned osseointegration as a possibility

CHAPTER 5

for some amputees but I'd been too blindsided by the more straight forward socket idea (that I assumed would be ideal) to have paid much attention. For the first time I began to wonder if osseointegration might be something that could work for me. All I really knew then was that it involved an implant of some sort.

I discovered that instead of making your bones weaker, as wearing sockets does, having a metal rod *implanted* into your bone (femur and tibia in my case) means you weight bear on living bone, which reactivates nerves and actually strengthens the bone. I liked that idea a lot.

Gradually as the bone marrow tissue and rod implant mesh together, you begin to get instant feedback to your brain that allows more natural and instinctive movement. Lower limb amputees really benefit from this technology enabling weight bearing onto the skeletal bones. The potential of technology for a person's physical recovery really is limitless.

I recalled Stefan had described various models of mechanical legs with different modes in them such as drive-mode, golf-mode, stiff leg-mode. I didn't think the laws here would allow use of the drive-mode but the implants were starting to sound much more flexible than the sockets. It just meant I would never be able to take the metal out. But who wants to take their legs off anyway?

After all the hiccups that I'd endured wearing the sockets

during my rehab phase, (imagine if I was to use the traditional sockets in the real world, I'd be running late to work every time, it's not like slipping on sandals!) I was keen to move forward with my plan and I contacted Stefan again who was very encouraging.

This was generous of him as it meant I wouldn't need his fabricating services for the prosthetics anymore. He put me in touch with the world's leading surgeon for osseointegration, Associate Professor Munjed Al Muderis, an Iraqi-born surgeon and refugee who had fled to Australia from the period of Hussein's tyranny.

My case manager for Lifetime Care, Judith Courts, was supportive of my idea too but warned me how difficult it would be to get the integration procedure approved, as they had never sanctioned such a technique before, they considered it to be quite new, unproven technology.

I thought I would just take it one step at a time, as I had to be assessed by the clinic first anyway before I applied to Lifetime Care. In December, I went along to one of Munjed's clinics in Sydney. It was a whole day process meeting Munjed and his team of different specialists who evaluated if I was a suitable candidate for the procedure. I met people who had come in for their check-ups having already had the procedure done and I met people like myself who had loads of questions to see if it was right for them.

CHAPTER 5

The physiotherapist thought I was a prime recipient. I was young, healthy, fit and would benefit significantly with procedures on both legs. They need to make sure you haven't lost your limbs to diabetes for example, as that condition is not ideal for the procedure to be a success.

I also saw a psychologist who had to probe deeply into how I would feel with metal rods sticking out of my body. In terms of appearance, you're literally sticking a foreign object into your body; they don't want you to wake up shocked! Little did they know of my appreciation for everything techno and mechanical. I had no doubts at all by then and was sure it was right for me.

I hadn't planned or even expected to want it so much, but I felt the road had definitely led me towards osseointegration for a reason. In the end the psychologist agreed I was a prime candidate and I 'passed' with flying colours. So my case manager Judith submitted my application in December and then we waited.

∿∿∿

We didn't have to wait long. Within a few weeks Lifetime Care replied with a big fat *"No"*. I wasn't completely surprised but

I was gutted, as somehow I just knew it would change my life. Judith explained it was a big sum for them to approve without having any precedent or evidence to support this technology in a largely untested commercial sense, it was just too risky to spend that sort of money up front.

Judith was tenacious though and told me not to give up. She went on a quest to gather as much information as possible in support of the procedure from a wider perspective. She collated data and compiled information supporting that it wasn't just a trial procedure but in fact has actually been around quite a while.

The idea behind modern osseointegration stemmed from dental implants in the 1960s and a lot of trial and error followed until they discovered the most compatible metallic implant is titanium, which resists corrosion and is not harmful or toxic to living tissue. Osseointegration has been successfully used clinically for amputees since 1995, improving rapidly with technological advancements.

An important argument Judith used to present our case was that currently amputees wearing sockets have to see a prosthetist regularly for new castings, in some cases it can be a few times a year which costs money every single time. Over five or ten years the cost could be even more than the surgical costs for osseointegration.

Judith submitted my application again with a whole team

CHAPTER 5

of people behind her who had endorsed the validity of the process. I was still so eager after being a perfect candidate. The ball was out of my court now and I had to believe in the evidence and information getting me over the line. I believed it could actually make a difference to other people who may find themselves in a similar situation one day too, I just happened to be the first. So I sent my wish out into the universe and tried to stay patient and positive.

My life had become very quiet and predictable again so after the success of my Vietnam trip, my friends thought we should do it all again and they convinced me to go to Hong Kong for a few weeks in February of 2014. They assured me they'd look after me and they thoughtfully arranged everything with my needs in mind.

Even though for my friends it was a party trip and they drank a fair bit, I was happy to chill and relax without feeling envious. I was rocking with my wheelchair at the time as I was definitely still not confident in walking with sockets in the real world. After all, it was really only during my rehab session that I had ever felt comfortable on two feet.

To risk walking in a foreign country where travel insurance might not even cover me if I were to hurt myself, I thought travelling in two wheels was just fine. I often turned in early to the hotel room while the others partied down at the bar; those days were well and truly over for me with no regrets.

My mind was preoccupied with my application to Lifetime Care. I even emailed them from the hotel lobby mid-holiday to check if there was any news. Nothing. I had to hold my breath a little bit longer.

> You are behind the wheel of your own journey. Cement those potholes so you enjoy the ride along the way.

CHAPTER 6

GO GO GADGET LEGS!

One week after arriving back in Sydney, I received the answer I had been hoping and praying for.

Lifetime Care had approved my osseointegration! After those agonising months wondering if I'd ever get this life-changing surgery, the phone call from Judith made me jump for joy! Maybe it was more like popping wheelies but when

CHAPTER 6

I told Mum, *man* she was over the moon, just so happy for me. The realisation dawned that I was going to be part robot. It consumed my every thought, like a countdown to an exciting race.

I knew it was going to be a long journey getting back on two feet but I had learnt long ago that fixing machines takes as long as it takes; it can't be rushed. Did I mention I was the first person Lifetime Care had ever approved for the procedure? I was also the 60th person Munjed had performed the surgery on and to date, the number of lucky recipients is around 1000 worldwide.

There was no hanging about either; it was all arranged for me to go into hospital for the first procedure on my right leg in March 2014. This right integration was surprisingly more straightforward than the shorter left integration would be. They could implant the rod directly into my right femur and then the microprocessor knee and leg component would be attached afterwards.

At one point the surgeon mentioned he should be able to smooth over some of the scarring as well, to tighten it up a bit. I was happy about this, as I was still self-conscious of the scarring at this point in time. In the end though Munjed thought it would be better to leave it as it was because after all, going into theatre was not to improve my appearance, (although I wouldn't say no to a surprise makeover) it was all about taking another huge step towards my independence.

I remember speaking to one of the patients in hospital about getting my skin refashioned. Surprised, she said to me, "What for? Why do you want to rewrite your story? It's there to remind you of what you've been through and shows the perseverance and determination to get where you are now. Be proud."

She reminded me that beauty can be found anywhere. My scars are now a symbol of my journey, like a notch honouring the hurdles I've overcome, they keep me grounded and grateful to be here.

∿∿∿

When I woke up from the procedure, there was no pain. Something in my body felt different but I was relaxed. I had pain medication on top of the epidural received in theatre to thank for that. My stump was all bandaged up like a Christmas present waiting to be unwrapped.

I was desperate to have a sneak peek under all those bandages but understood it was significant surgery and I knew I had to resist being that eager kid who opens their presents early or I'd end up on Santa's naughty list.

CHAPTER 6

It took a couple of days of wondering before my new limb was at long last revealed. I thought the metal poking through the stump looked amazing. Any doubts I had leftover from my socket-wearing days were instantly negated.

Just thinking about the freedom and comfort I would experience once I became accustomed to my new means of walking, had me bouncing with excitement like a puppy desperate to fetch that tennis ball. I had to control my eagerness though because they wouldn't let me try too much too fast.

The physios explained I had to slowly increase the all-important weight bearing aspect. Using a hoist, I would lean onto the scales on my abutment (the short metal piece protruding from the stump) until it read 5kgs and the physios would hold me in place for around ten minutes at a time. It went up incrementally each day until I was leaning 50% of my body weight onto the scale. I was fatter by then, I'd regained a lot of weight which was a good thing.

Everything went so well in fact that I was only in hospital for two weeks. For those amputees who have been using sockets for decades, it takes a lot longer for the bone to recognise and respond after so long without weight bearing nerves being activated. I was young and fit so my body responded quickly to the integration.

I wasn't hopping around on one leg when I got home aka

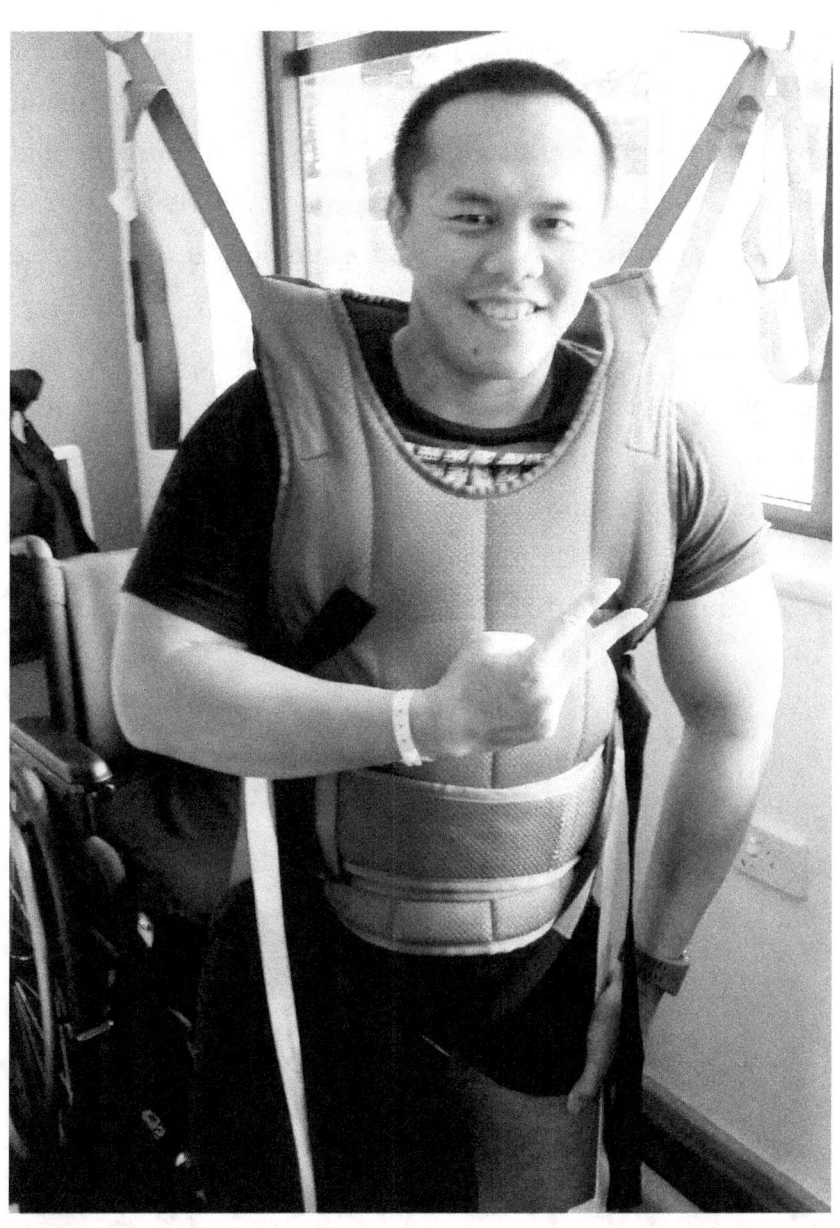

Hoist for weight bearing on my left knee, it gave me such a wedgy.

CHAPTER 6

'Pogo Khoa'. I would have to wait for the microprocessor knee attachment first. So yes that meant that I was once again bound to the wheelchair, not that it was a bad thing. I could scoot around and show off my flashy metal, and boy it sure did pull a lot of curiosity. After all how often do you see someone with a metal rod sticking out of their leg?

I was already looking forward to the next procedure on my left leg. Munjed had explained the left leg was more complicated due to the short length of tibia I had left below the knee. There was not enough bone below the knee for the implant. So I needed a knee replacement first, which was then used to integrate with the femur above the knee and the tibia

Out with the socket in with the implant – no looking back now.

below the knee, it was a fully custom designed knee so would take longer to manufacture.

For a short time I considered asking them for an amputation above the knee so I could simply get another microprocessor knee like my right one. But I still have control of my left knee, even if it's only a 10-degree bend; it's still *my* movement controlling it. Munjed also explained that this idea created the risk of complications arising. Keeping things ticking over just fine was actually a really positive decision.

∿∿∿

Only two weeks after arriving home, I was surprised to wake up one morning feeling weaker than normal. I assumed it was from DOMS (Delayed Onset Muscle Soreness) from training with heavier weights but it was hard to pinpoint the feeling exactly. Just a bit floppy, not much strength when I tried to grip something but otherwise I felt fine. I thought I must have trained too hard the day before and my body was telling me to slow down.

I was still battling acne at that time and in an effort to get rid of it I had stopped drinking my protein supplements that helped me gain more muscle. So I wondered if removing the

CHAPTER 6

protein had affected my muscle strength.

The next day was the same, except this time I really noticed that I couldn't even do the mundane things like pick up a coffee cup, zip my jacket up or use chopsticks. I checked 'Dr Google' and I admit I was mildly worried about the possibilities.

Mum drove me to the GP who assessed me with questions. Bewildered as to what I was explaining to him, he decided to arrange for me to go see a specialist. In another moment of good fortune, within two weeks I was able to squeeze into an appointment with the neurologist at Macquarie University Hospital. These appointments usually take three months or more.

The day arrived and I was happy to get to the bottom of this strange, sudden weakness. The specialist undertook some reflex tests from my elbows down to my hands, checking for good reactions to his prodding.

I failed the tests. All the symptoms pointed in one direction. I was diagnosed with Guillain-Barre Syndrome. Symptoms for this condition usually start in the legs so this had made diagnosis less straightforward in my case when I had thought my arms were just weak from over training. I was grateful the doctor acted on his suspicion so quickly.

You might be able to guess what came next. Yes, it was straight off to hospital for me once again. I was the *one* in the

1 in 100,000 people that get Guillain-Barre Syndrome, lucky guy or what - wish it were the lottery!

Man! My life was becoming stranger than fiction. Doctors don't know exactly what causes Guillain-Barre Syndrome; it can sometimes occur after a bacterial or viral infection or occasionally after a surgery.

It's an auto-immune disorder so my nerves cells were being attacked from within and creating weakness in my muscles. For some people they never fully recover and it can be fatal for a small percentage of sufferers as well. It was a pretty scary time wondering which category I would fit into.

The hospital part I didn't mind though, I saw it as a chance to spread my humour to those hard-working, underappreciated professionals who work in a pretty sombre environment. The staff can get a bit mellow and sad and I see it as my duty to lighten their load, make them smile, make their day more enjoyable, that's what I'm good at.

This time I was admitted to the Royal Northshore Hospital for treatment, so it was another adventure going to a new hospital, spreading joy to new people. It's my nature to have fun wherever I go, even in hospital, strange but true.

So even though it was a serious condition I was fairly comfortable while I recovered. To treat Guillain-Barre Syndrome they put me on a 5-day course of immunoglobulin therapy via an intravenous drip based on my blood type.

CHAPTER 6

I only needed five days in hospital but it took me almost three months to get back to normal, which was surely still another thing to be grateful for. I returned to rehab and gradually noticed my strength returning. Each day I would check the counter on my handgrips to measure the strength of my grip. I made a full recovery.

∿∿∿

It felt amazing to get home after another close call. I could concentrate on getting ready for the next integration. Munjed recommended we should wait for three months to make sure the Guillain-Barre treatment was fully out of my system before embarking on the next, bigger procedure.

I didn't see this as a setback as I didn't have a set date in mind to be magically 'healed'. I knew I could only make small steps according to what my body needed. However I was certain it would happen.

While I was at home waiting for the next integration, I realised I was thinking about Tonee a lot and that it was time to go and see him. For almost a year after the accident, Tonee's mum had not let anyone come and see him and I didn't even know exactly where he was for a long time.

I can only imagine how difficult it was for her to accept the consequences of the accident and I understand it was her way of protecting Tonee and processing what happened. Eventually she let his friends visit and reconnect with him again.

I wasn't sure how I would feel or react when I saw him the first time; would I talk to him normally? Would I burst out in anger? The minute I saw him when I rolled in with my wheelchair, I felt only happiness that my friend was still with us. I could see in his eyes that he knew me, and that he was just locked up in his human shell.

I felt relieved at my reaction, that deep down I had let it go and didn't hold on to any past actions. If I did, that would have meant Tonee would be living rent free in my head and I was having none of that!

I've seen Tonee regularly ever since. I try not to let too much time go by without seeing him and I know he loves it when I walk in with his favourite takeaway food for him. It's hard to know if he remembers how he ended up in the nursing home. One day the nurse asked him if he knew who I was and he managed to say my name. Another time he managed a few chess moves before he became too tired to play with me.

A few friends and I also took Tonee and his carer out for the day to a car show at Homebush stadium. I could see Tonee's eyes darting around everywhere trying to take it all

CHAPTER 6

in. He still loves cars too and his smile that day said it all.

Along with seeing Tonee, I had been worried about seeing the same model car as the accident: Would it trigger a flashback of the accident? A light switch bringing it all back to make me sad? Luckily no.

When I first saw the same model car again on the road, I just appreciated it because of my love of cars. I was a passenger in one too eventually, but I felt fine. The truth is I still don't remember anything from the accident and I'll look at it as a positive sign from a negative situation.

∿∿∿

I was feeling great again and was all set for my second integration on September 5th. Thankfully it all went smoothly just like the first procedure. I consider this to be the start of my real independence, my new life. I was happy to do rehab for as long as I needed to because I knew this would be for the long haul.

Since I had been relying on my wheelchair for a period of time leading up to the left leg integration, my leg muscles were not very active. Always being seated causes your hip flexors to tighten so the physiotherapists made sure I was

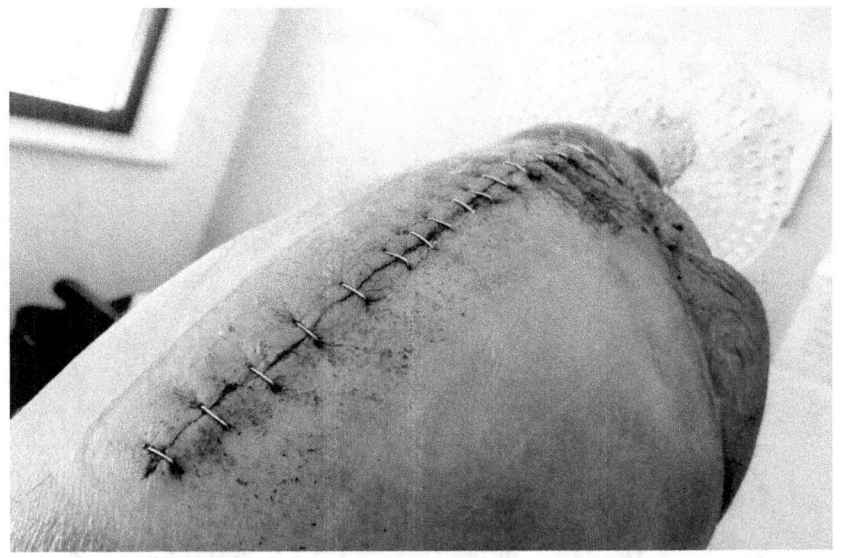
The necessary left knee replacement to go along with the implant.

An advanced move in fitness – the planche – yeah, I have an advantage.

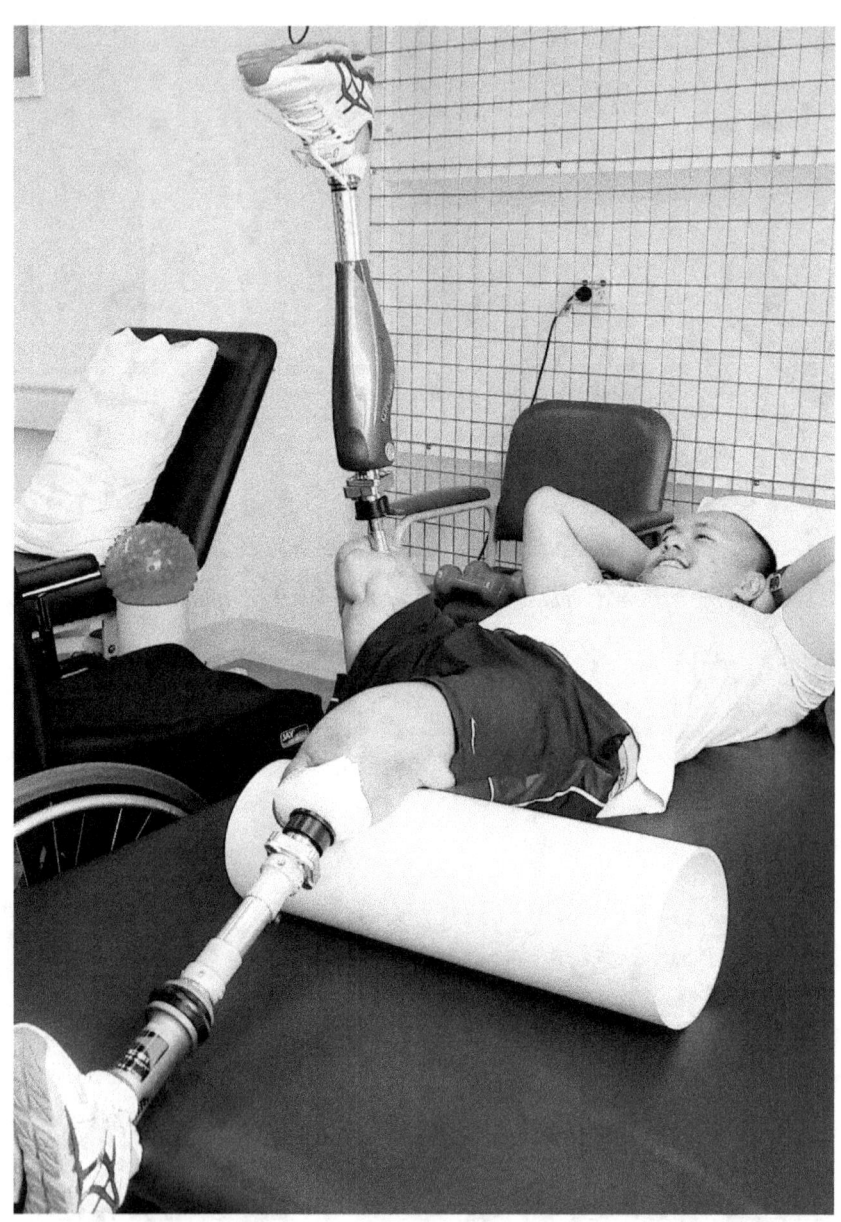

I definitely make people look twice, a limited edition piece.

focusing on building up my gluteal muscles. Me being me, I couldn't resist making the most out of those arse training sessions with my usual humour. Vertical smile anyone?

The left connector hadn't arrived yet so while I couldn't walk without both connectors, I could at least finally connect my right leg. I was halfway there. I could use my right leg attachment to help build strength while I was lying on the physio bed. It was also handy for pulling pranks on unsuspecting patients. Honestly, who can rotate their foot 180 degrees while doing leg raises?

I was getting a bit too comfortable in the hospital while waiting for the left connector (I'll take active over idle any day) so I thought it was best to go home and return again when it was ready. I was sad to leave the nurses and therapists who'd been with me from the start of my rehab but I consoled them that they would see my pretty face again soon enough.

The exciting phone call from Stefan came six days later, to say the left connector had arrived. I bubbled with excitement as we drove to Stefan's clinic in Northmead. Mum and my brother came with me to share the big moment.

Stefan used a red laser to align the leg so it matched my position and stance perfectly. He connected the male/female coupling of the connector and leg and then I was able to push myself up from the wheelchair and support my weight between the parallel bars.

CHAPTER 6

I stood up for the first time and looked in the mirror. I was completely overwhelmed. For once I could barely speak.

I was finally on two feet, without sockets, standing tall like I did before, taller even! All I could say was, "Wow, wow, wow!" I hadn't been fully vertical for 10 months since my last skin break from the sockets. I felt dizzy from the strange height!

My legs felt immediately comfortable, I knew there was nothing surrounding my thighs, it felt liberating and life-changing. No need to spend ten minutes putting these on and funnily enough I was relieved to think how much easier it would be sitting on the toilet without a bulky socket getting in the way! Ha ha!

I felt so different from that funny but slightly lost, irresponsible guy I was in my twenties, now I felt so much power and purpose in my life. I could take it to a new level, my world was opening up full of possibilities as long as I took my time and focused on each single step in front of me — literally.

Even though I had dreamed of this for so long, it was such a surreal experience because if you wind back to the year before, I had been cruising on two wheels building up my arms all day long propelling myself around. If my arms got lazy, I had my brother or mother to push me, a luxury I sometimes took for granted.

This time, that support had reduced dramatically, but fortunately my big bulging arms had not. I could learn to do everything myself. Not a bad trade off at all.

I wasn't allowed to simply start strutting around. I would have to go into hospital for at least two weeks rehab. So I kept them on but stayed in the wheelchair for the time being. I tried little experiments to see what I could do, exercised with them lying on the ground or went to the park to test myself on the parallel bars.

My excitement was building as I happily returned to rehab in hospital. I know, right? Who actually looks forward to staying in the hospital for two weeks? It's the last place anyone wants to be. But this stay was the most exciting of all my admissions to hospital because it finally meant I could learn to walk again. So if you were in my shoes, you'd think the same. Plus I also got to torment those nurses again with my hilarious jokes.

All of my missing pieces were ready!

Rehab was all about repetition, learning how to engage what muscles when. Hour after hour, day after day, it was slow but steady progress. Soon I was ready to go home as an outpatient. I had been waiting for this day for so long. Picture me wearing rock star sunglasses, strutting away on two crutches before turning back to wave goodbye to my crew and then sliding into my limousine.

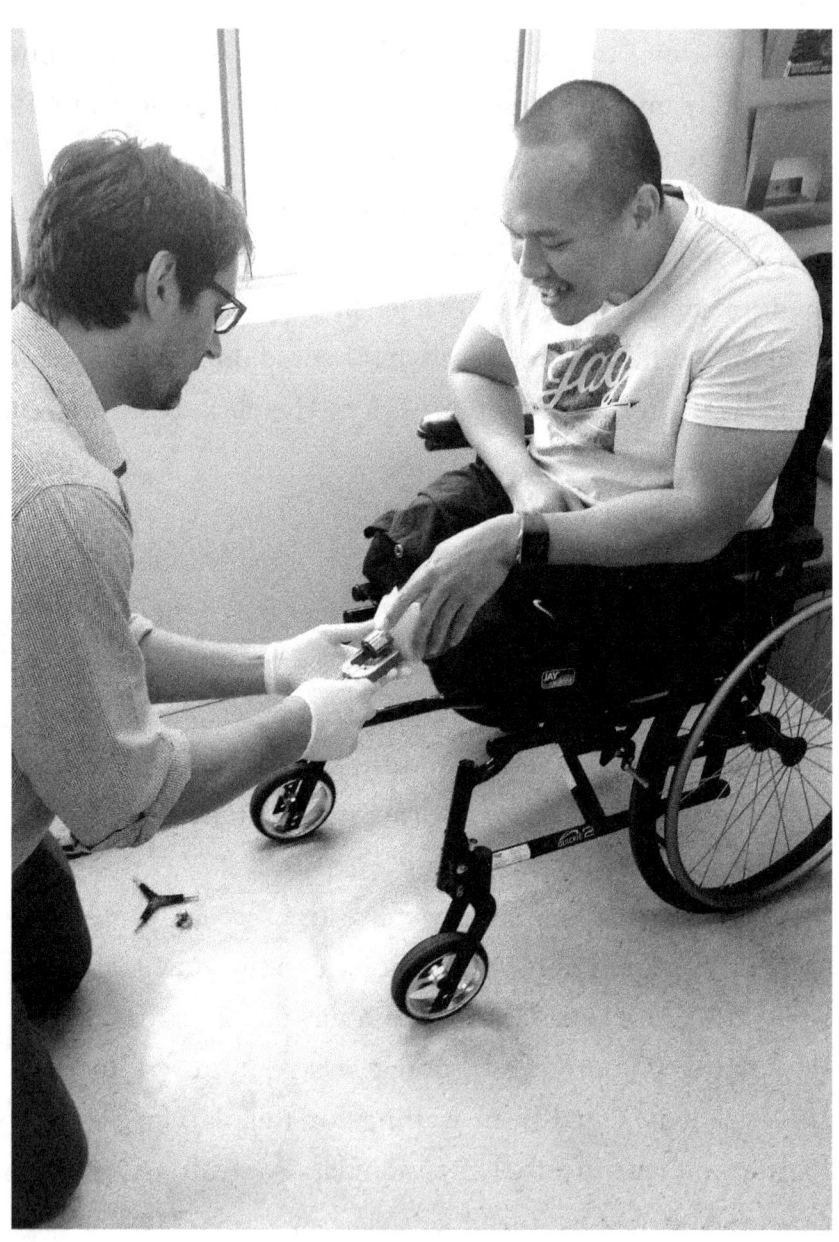

Stefan had the honour of completing the jigsaw puzzle.

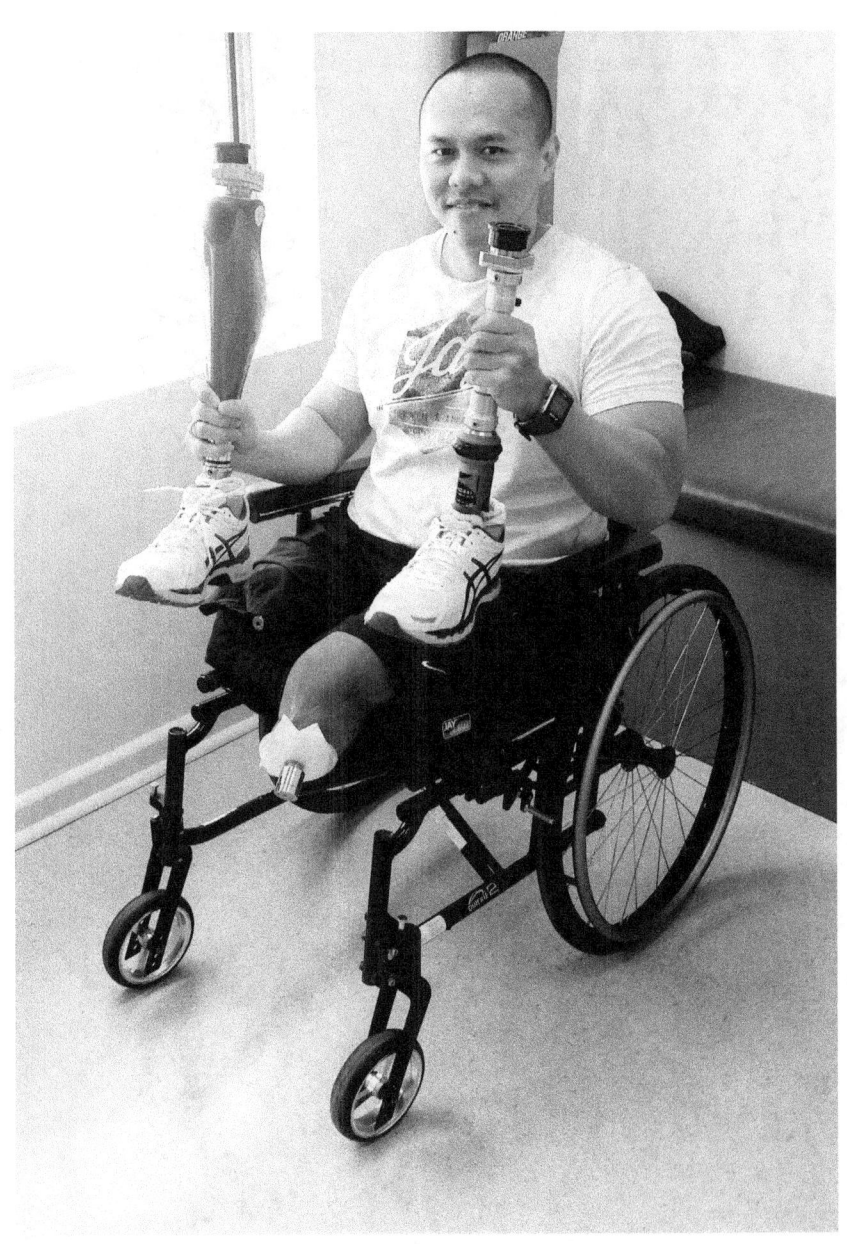

Finally I'm complete.

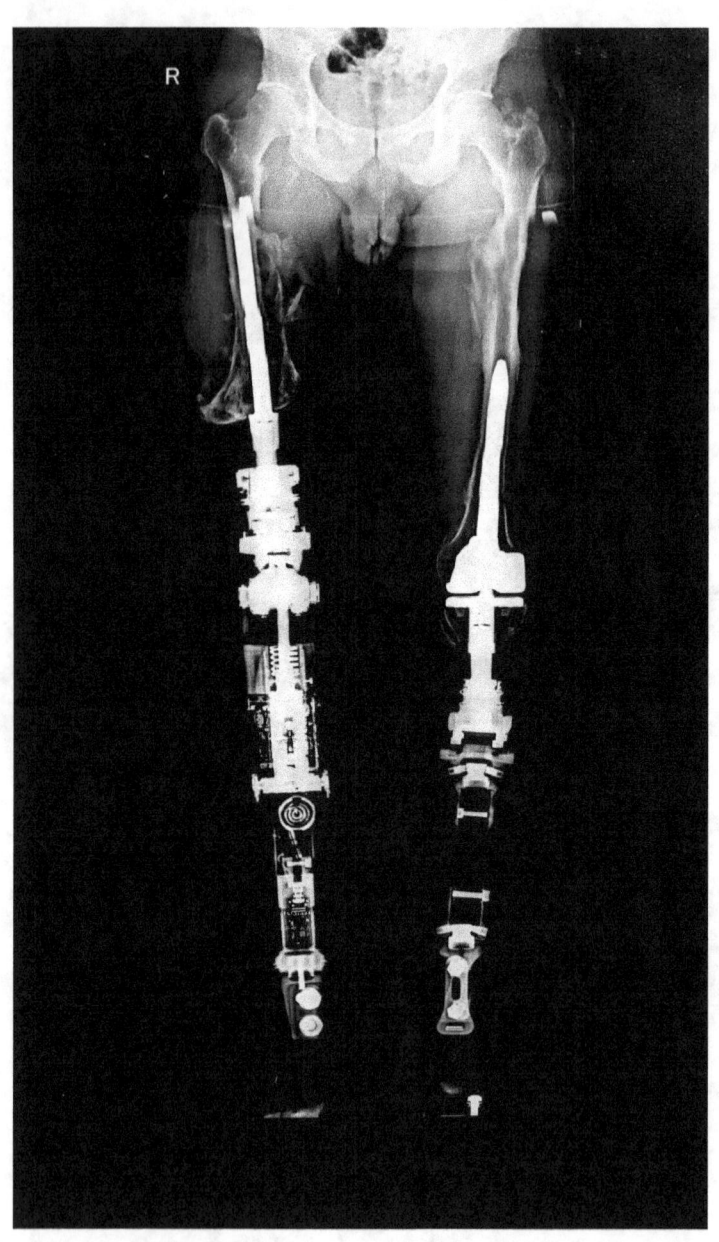

Now tell me this isn't cool!

GO GO GADGET LEGS

I felt like that on the inside but the reality wasn't anywhere near that image. To be on the safe side, I wheeled myself out to the car park with my legs packed away in a bag, swinging myself into the car like I was used to. Not quite a rock star exit but nevertheless I was about to embrace the most exciting chapter of my journey.

∿∿∿

Once home, I had to somehow convert my house layout into a rehab environment so I replaced the parallel bars with the hallway walls leading into the kitchen. I would place my

Rehab never stops.

CHAPTER 6

palms hard against the wall to walk back and forth, increasing my step counts and strength.

The temptation of the kitchen being at one end proved challenging. My well-planned home rehab session would often end up as a one-way path to the fridge but don't worry, that chocolate éclair was worth the distraction: a reward for being able to get it myself.

I returned to the gym and enjoyed showing off my new legs, many people had never seen me on two feet, only in the wheelchair. It took time to get the hang of walking; I would need both crutches for nearly a year before I started to feel a natural balance from the integration.

By February of 2015 I felt ready to take another trip to Vietnam for a friend's wedding, this time with legs. Walking myself down the plane aisle to my seat was a big milestone right there. I know it sounds like an ordinary action, but I'm not ordinary - just take a look.

In Vietnam, I was very cautious when I walked around, the last thing I needed was to fall over and break myself again. When we got there I was so pumped to show off my new walk to my relatives. They had never connected with me at eye level and Mum wanted to show them how far I'd come since they last saw me.

That wasn't the only thing that I surprised them with. My cystic acne was in full swing by then and my once flawless

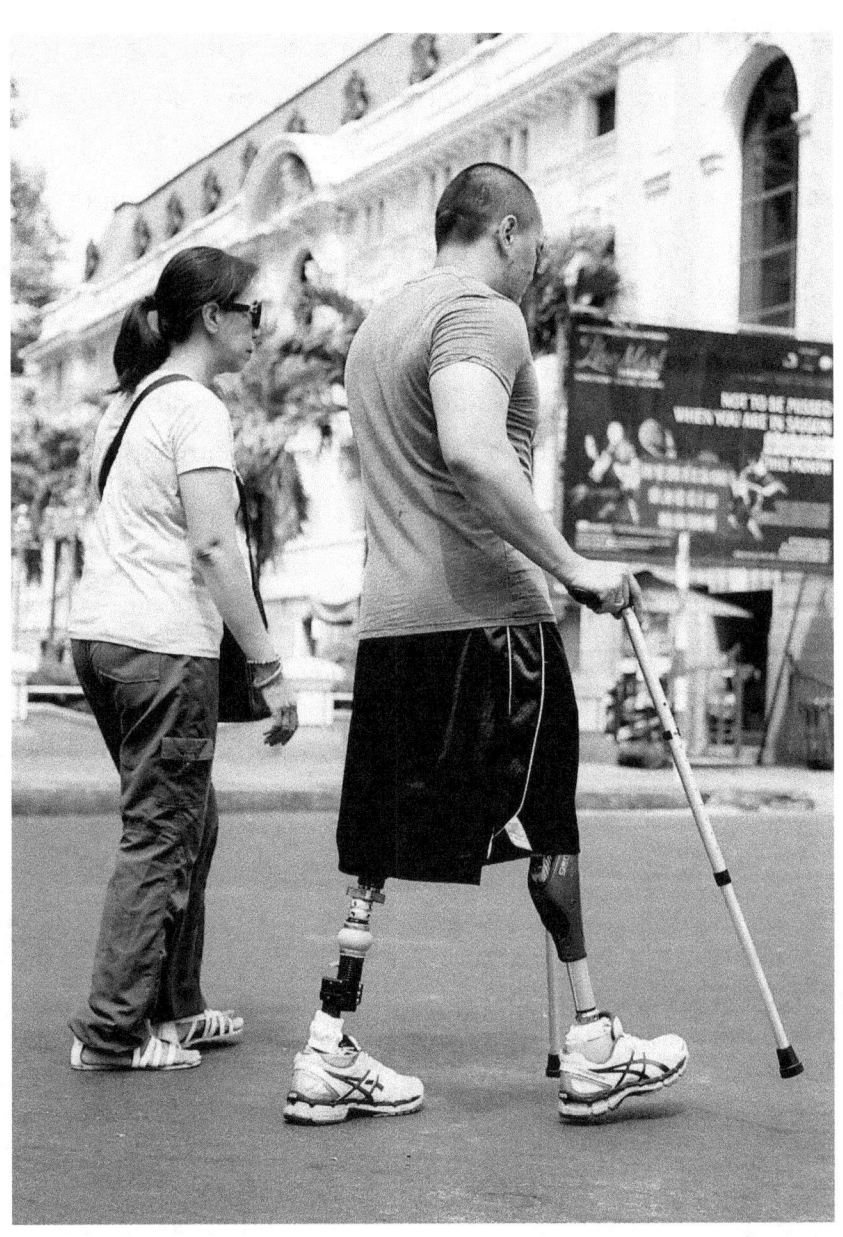

Second visit to Vietnam on all fours in Ho Chi Minh City.

CHAPTER 6

face had lots of active volcanoes and scarring. I guess you can't have everything right? I'm thankful that the course of medication prescribed by my dermatologist would slowly but surely ease the unusual outbreaks I was going through then.

It was my first time attending a wedding overseas and what a way to experience learning how to walk again. Walking along the streets of Rạch Giá in my uncomfortable formal attire, sweating in the humidity, while concentrating on my every step surely made another memorable imprint on my topsy-turvy journey.

Come to think of it, it was a mix of humidity and laser-intense concentration that made me sweat, as I commanded myself, *"Don't trip over Khoa, don't - trip -over!"*

〰〰〰

By late 2015 I had ditched one of my walking sticks, the balance of the internal integration was becoming second nature to me. I kept improving every day and was notching up so many steps, I felt ready and excited to take a road trip with my friends up to Queensland and camp at Fraser Island.

Some fun facts about Fraser Island; beautiful wild dingoes roam the beaches there scavenging for scraps left by inattentive tourists and Fraser Island is also the largest sand island in the world. Yes, you read that right — *sand*.

Now it's hard enough for an able bodied person to walk on soft sand, so you can imagine how my robot legs and I handled it - fun times. I was actually interested to test myself and see if I could manage the off-road terrain and tick it off my list of achievements.

Let me tell you though, the mental patience required to stay motivated while you watch each step sink deeply into the sand repeatedly makes you want to give up with every type of exhaustion but I had overcome worse things in life, so I decided not to let a bit of sand stop me.

My independence was blossoming, experiencing life again this time with metal legs. The step counter on my robotic legs was getting some serious usage; even Stefan was astounded by how much I walked. So how would I finish off my camping trip to one of the most pristine islands in the world?

By jumping off a plane of course!

I wanted to relive that feeling of invincibility from when I skydived in 2009. I even wanted to feel those heart palpitations again from free falling out of a plane at 14,000ft. They were as thrilling as I remembered. It felt like I'd come full circle back to some sort of 'normal' to be lucky enough to relive the exact same feeling of being on top of the world — only this time my legs weren't with me.

CHAPTER 6

I handed them off to the staff so that when we landed on the beach, they would be armed - or should I say 'legged' - ready to hand them over, or should that be 'foot' them over - so my alter ego, the T800 could be reassembled.

Wait — were you worried I was reminiscing about my actual legs that I hadn't seen since 2012? Nah, these legs are much cooler, I get to upgrade them and did I mention they're detachable? Ha ha.

Skydiving in Noosa. The adrenalin in me never stopped.

Despite achieving life-changing progress, I still wasn't fully independent. I didn't have a driver's licence and relied on my family and friends for anywhere I wanted to go. I realised that I would have to take the plunge and go for my licence. I can hear you asking, *"Why didn't you pursue this earlier? After all, you're obsessed with cars."*

I've thought about this a lot and after the accident I assumed driving again might not be possible and so I accepted it and moved on. I didn't want to dwell on what I had 'lost', only on what I had gained in this new life.

If I'm honest though, deep down I knew driving was an option that I had been scared to explore. I simply didn't want to drive a hand control car or be tied to just one car. I suppose I was hanging onto my past here and was hesitant to taint my good memories of being behind the wheel, which were some of the best times of my youth in fact.

I always loved sliding into different cars and taking them for a test drive, it was a passion that I lived for. I appreciated feeling the different sounds and movements of the cars as a driver and absorbing the way they handled on the road. Driving would never be the same again and was one of the

CHAPTER 6

hardest things for me to accept. I had shut myself off from thinking and talking about driving again.

However as my compensation payout came through in 2015, I realised my future was waiting for me and it would be much easier if I could get myself around again. I knew it was the right thing for my independence. It was the last piece of my past that I finally let go of.

Once I had made that decision, I full accepted that if driving again meant driving a hand control car, so be it. I would do whatever I had to for my future to begin.

The occupational therapist and driving instructor came to my house soon after and we chatted about my situation. Firstly they needed me to undertake memory and awareness tests, both of which I aced by the way. Next we discussed control options such as rings or levers.

I remembered Stefan telling me about a drive setting on my titanium legs back in the early days when driving was just a vague dream for the future. Simply out of interest, I mentioned to the instructor that my leg had a driving mode and I showed them some videos on my iPad of people using the driving mode in America. The OT and instructor were both amazed — they hadn't known that was an option.

Then came some unexpected and incredible news.

"We can do this!" they cried.

What! I was stunned. I had assumed it wouldn't even

Watch out guys! I'm back!

be a faint possibility here in Australia because of safety or legalities or something. I had never even dreamed to aim that high. Discovering that my integration meant I could drive an unmodified car was an amazing highlight in my recovery. My family and friends were so happy for me too, knowing how

CHAPTER 6

much it meant that I could get back behind the wheel and put my 'foot' to the metal!

To begin with it meant I could only drive automatic cars but I could live with that. To drive a manual transmission I would need a modified duck clutch where the clutch lever is installed on the gear stick. I filed that information away for a future date.

I took one driving lesson in a hand-control car just to ease back into it. But once Stefan inserted the drive mode setting into the app on my phone that controls my legs, I was off. That first time behind the wheel was incredible; I felt like a kid, *"Look at me everyone!"*

I admit there was a learning curve judging the spacing between the pedals. I put some padding next to my thighs so I wouldn't go too far to the right and potentially miss the pedal. I learnt really quickly how to shift my hips slightly right-to-left, left-to-right, to get the movement I needed. This is where the integration really showed its ingenuity and worth by providing instantaneous feedback straight up from my 'foot' resting on the accelerator up into my living bone, it was seamless.

I passed my licence with flying colours in my instructor's car, highest of the highest scores. The assessor didn't feel any difference at all in the driving or performance of the car than with conventional drivers.

It felt strange and a little ironic to be back driving my mum's car around again, I was ready to go to the runs again ...*joking*! I took a few trips just for the fun of it, practising and enjoying driving again or randomly turning up at a friend's house just because I could.

I loved being back behind the wheel and best of all was surprising people when they saw a driver climb out with no legs. They couldn't be more stunned than if a monkey had climbed out of the driver's seat, the looks on their faces were priceless.

∿∿∿

Another exciting moment came in mid 2016, when I received my shower legs. You might wonder what's so exciting about that? Well, ever since I came home from hospital, I needed to use a self-propelled commode chair for the toilet and shower.

After osseointegration, I didn't need to rely on it for toilet duties anymore but that didn't mean I could put it aside. I still needed to shower and my legs were definitely not waterproof so I would use the commode chair for showering only. Now here comes the tricky part.

When I went to Vietnam (on both occasions), we didn't want to lug the commode because it wasn't a collapsible item

CHAPTER 6

you can store away on a plane. Every hotel that we stayed at did its best to accommodate a person with a disability but if there were no disabled-access rooms, then I would have to look for any type of furniture to use. Whether that be a plastic chair, a stool, or even a small cupboard, I had to improvise with my surroundings.

Surely if the health and safety officer saw how I had showered, they would have had nightmares. Hey, not everything is served on a silver platter; sometimes you've gotta be like *MacGyver* in this modern world and improvise.

Remember I had been putting up with boring 'baths' in the hospital with wipes and water and then shallow baths at home. Those are pretty dull compared to the absolute luxury of being able to stand up and feel tingling hot water cascade over you from your head to your robot toes. Standing tall and independently in my own shower is something I will never take for granted again. I was feeling pretty pleased with myself in my sexy shower legs.

My days were getting busier again as I was moving and walking around more freely. I had lost weight since the integration from my new mobility. I was also going to the gym again as I loved feeling fit and I knew it was the best way to gain the full benefit from my integration.

I believe I have fitness to thank for me being alive today. If I hadn't built up a strong heart and strong muscles from those years of mountain biking and going to the gym, I doubt I would have been strong enough to survive the accident and resulting surgeries.

Fitness has always been a part of my life and I believe it not only gave me a much better chance of being approved for the osseointegration but also being able to physically recover to such an empowering point that I'm at today.

Throughout 2016 a possibility had been growing in my mind that I was finally ready for the next big step in my life. An opportunity came along to buy into a gym business and I felt a spark light up immediately. It suited everything I loved, fitness, meeting new people and supporting them with a smile whenever they needed it.

I talked to my brother who was interested too and we were able to form a partnership with another mate to buy a gym franchise in a great location in Sydney in early 2017.

Since then I have become the face of the gym. I'm there almost every day and I love the happy environment we've created. I'm great at encouraging everyone to keep striving for their fitness goals. We take pride in our presentation and

CHAPTER 6

cleanliness and our members love coming here.

I have a few staff to manage but mostly we are just friends that have fun together. I do have a 'boss voice' in case you're wondering, but rarely have to use it. Occasionally I need a hand with something and I'm not too proud to ask for help, if the job needs doing, I just do it any way I can.

Managing the gym was a new chapter in independence

Guess the plates …

and I felt really fulfilled at the end of each day. I obtained my Personal Training Certificate and I also got a certificate as a physio aid. I couldn't keep borrowing Mum's car to drive to my TAFE courses so I went car hunting planning on buying a Toyota Corolla. A friend came with me and convinced me to try an Audi dealership.

It was my first and last stop. This car was certainly a big difference to what I had been planning but I now take this baby on the racetrack whenever I can afford it, as my thrill for speed has never disappeared. She's modified, but I don't mean hand controls, you know me — performance mods.

∿∿

Once I had my licence, I was totally enjoying the fun and freedom of life again and was rarely at home. Mum would call me to ask me where I was and if I was coming home, she liked to know I was safe at home. I would sometimes still party to the morning but my energy came from gratitude for being there, not desire for alcohol or blacked out memories. How lucky did I feel!

One exciting opportunity seemed to lead to another. For example in July 2017, I innocently went along to a two-day event about how to grow your business, never imagining it would open up a whole new world and a new direction for me. After the business speaker finished talking, a guest speaker appeared on stage who immediately caught my interest because he had a prosthetic arm and his leg was fused at the knee.

His name was Sam Cawthorn and he had been in a horrendous car accident in 2006. His right arm had to be amputated and he was left with a permanent disability in his right leg. Sam's message about 'bouncing forward' really connected with me and I could see elements of that in how I had never given up. Sam gave me confidence that maybe my story was worth sharing too.

Ever since I started recovering from my accident people had often said to me, "You're amazing Khoa … you haven't let anything stop you from getting on with life … you're an inspiration … you should share your story … spread your message … talk to school kids."

The truth is though; I had never tried to inspire anyone. Since my accident I had simply tried to live the best I could by constantly moving forward, not looking back asking pointless questions. Listening to Sam helped me to see my journey in a much clearer light, and I asked myself if what people had been telling me for years was true then maybe I really could inspire people to overcome big battles in their lives.

How great would that be, I thought, *to use my story for such a good cause as helping other people?* I've always enjoyed making people smile and if I could do that on a bigger scale, using my experiences to make a real difference to how they live their lives and battle their challenges, that would be a dream come true, one that I didn't even know was possible.

Sam's confident presence made a big impression on me and I remembered the way the whole audience responded in awe at his personal triumph and his force of hope and strength in the face of adversity. As soon as he walked on stage I could see he had a powerful story to share; if a man with one arm could make that kind of impact straight off the bat, then what were my possibilities I wondered.

The kid in me pictured making an entrance on stage in an all-out Terminator makeover, red laser eyes and all.

∿∿∿

I was so excited to think I could help in a whole new way but I was also nervous because I knew it would take a lot of work and practice for me to learn to talk on stage like Sam. I'd harboured a secret fear for many years about public speaking. I loved holding people's attention as I joked around but to be looking out at a crowd sharing the raw, honest version of what

CHAPTER 6

I'd been through, I knew I would have to level up big time.

After signing up to more of Sam's programs, he helped me to dissect *how* I had achieved all I had since the accident. We identified certain traits I utilise to keep me moving forward away from sadness or regret. That's not to say I'm immune to these feelings but I'm pretty quick to tell them where to shove it.

That's my whole mindset, to always look for the positive in negative-looking situations, no matter how small the positive is, it'll get bigger the more you focus on it.

To give you another example, I had been hoping that one day, my left knee could be manipulated into a greater degree of flexibility. It had only been left with a 10-degree bend for nearly three years due to Heterotopic Ossification (HTO), which is the abnormal growth of bone in non-skeletal tissues, tendons and muscles.

After the accident, the bend in my left knee became so limited I couldn't tuck my foot fully underneath me when I sat down. There were a few times sitting in a waiting room, when my socket leg 'accidentally' tripped people over and they took a little unintended tumble. My osseointegration has actually saved many a person from any cheeky temptation of mine, because now I can literally take off my leg in mere seconds to prevent any embarrassing (yet humorous) trips. The glares have turned into curious stares instead.

Munjed likes to wait at least a good three years for the HTO to settle before they try any manipulation. If you disrupt it too early, it will grow even more. So it was actually three years down the track before I was finally all set to go under again and have the manipulation done. When I woke up I was expecting to feel pain. The fact there wasn't any gave me a hint at what the surgeon was going to say.

When he came in he served the news up straight; it didn't work, it was just too risky. They had tried to bend it, but the procedure involves forcing it to crack and there was just too much calcification formed behind the knee that they didn't want to risk damaging what wasn't broken.

I sat there disappointed for a moment; it meant I couldn't ride a bike again, not an unmodified bike anyway. But my next thought was clear as crystal. *You know what? That's fine, these three years have been great and I'm just gonna do what I can with what I have, no dwelling on what can't be.*

I accepted it and moved on to more important things; what *could* be.

> Smile at that stranger or have a laugh with that colleague because your simple act of connection can lift someone's whole world.

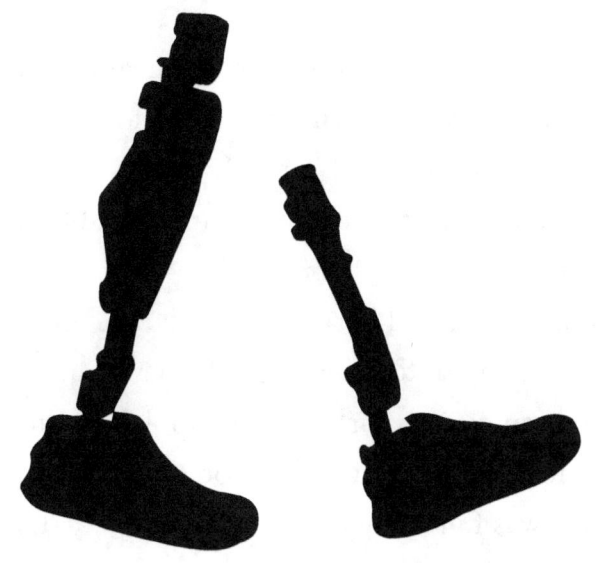

CHAPTER 7
LEVELLING UP

Have you heard of the saying, "To get over your fear you have to face it"?

Not long after my amputations, I was still self-conscious about my legs, afraid of people judging me. On one of my early ventures out in public, I made sure my legs were well-covered; protective sleeves covered the bandages and then I concealed

CHAPTER 7

them *further* with long shorts tucked beneath my legs hoping to deter people from throwing me weird looks.

This was in vain and later I would come to realise, unnecessary. Plenty of looks came my way and I thought, *Gee, this is gonna take a bit to get used to!*

Next a mother and her child noticed me and the kid just came straight up and asked me, "What happened to your legs?" His mum was mortified and apologised to me but it was actually the best thing that could have happened. The child's face was full of innocence and curiosity; there was no judgment there at all.

This was a light blub moment for me, giving me the courage to be open and honest with anyone that wants to ask about my story. Unfiltered as kids are, I knew it was right to let him know what had happened. I could've made an awesome story out of this situation (saving my dog from a shark attack sounds like a cool narrative) but I'll leave the fibs to those smooth talking, slippery guys arguing over policies in the media.

This boy and his natural, friendly curiosity really helped me to overcome my fear of facing people in public and what they might say. Everyone feels more comfortable not skirting around the elephant in the room and I think adults have the same curiosity but feel it's rude to ask.

Maybe some people feel offended but for me I am now

happy to share my story with curious people and show them that despite it looking like I've lost something, I haven't! I actually have more than I did before.

∿∿∿

So back to the fear dilemma, if I wanted to pursue my new passion to share my story on a wider platform and help other people, I knew I'd have to face my fear of public speaking. I was comfortable showing my legs off by that time but I would have to jump out of my comfort zone in order to talk confidently and tell my story on stage.

Sam Cawthorn had become a big mentor for me and I followed on with his teachings by joining his yearlong program of boot camps and a whole curriculum coaching me in how to connect and make the impact I was hoping for. One effective strategy is not just telling the story but revealing the raw emotion of it, this makes a lasting impact.

I loved raising my confidence from joking around with friends to sharing meaningful stories on stage. On the final night of the boot camp, I was still pretty nervous about presenting my talk to the coaches. My heart pounded in my throat before I went on stage but once I took that first

CHAPTER 7

steadying breath to break the ice, I flowed with incredible energy.

I met great people from all walks of life on this program and I was so impressed by their stories too. Some presented their talks with slides, videos and backdrops, which added a new angle that I really appreciated from a technical point of view. The coaches gave us feedback before we were asked to present our talks again on the last day.

So in typical teenager style, I spent all day Saturday madly adding my new idea of visual concepts to my final presentation, it felt like cramming for an exam you haven't studied for! Our final appearance on stage was a culmination of 12 months of learning and exploring the deepest parts of our journeys. The final applause went on for ages; we were celebrating each other and ourselves too.

∿∿

Through Sam's program there was an opportunity to apply for one of ten spots at a TENx talk. This was a really big deal and so I nervously prepared a one-minute video to apply, as did 60 other people.

I wasn't expecting it but was ecstatic when I was chosen to

be one of the ten speakers. This was a huge milestone for me, presenting to more than 160 guests from around the world at the Sea World Resort on the Gold Coast. I shared the stage with the likes of Dale Beaumont, Lisa McInnes-Smith and Ruth Saw just to name a few.

An early talk to my biggest international crowd, I felt at home. Photo credit John Lee.

CHAPTER 7

I didn't stop there. Without working on my confidence with Sam, I would never have had the courage to apply for a special TV show in 2018 called *Taboo*[3]. Through the NSW Amputee Association I found out about a media opportunity with a production company that was planning something a little unusual and they were searching for four open-minded people with a disability.

I was intrigued so even though I didn't know the full story I tried my luck and applied. Through the course of the interviews they explained the Australian comedian Harley Breen wanted to lift some of the misconceptions around disability by sharing our stories on a personal but *humorous* level, discussing everything that people are afraid to ask.

I realised I could be a voice for the disabled community and I admired his idea to use humour to engage the audience. My application was successful and I was so excited to head off with Harley, the TV crew and the other participants for a week's holiday in the Southern Highlands of New South Wales.

The retreat allowed us to get to know one another in a relaxed, open way. We spent time talking to Harley about the challenges we deal with every day just like everyone else. Harley would perform a stand-up comedy routine for our family and friends the following week that showed our real selves with sensitivity, respect and loads of humour so we could laugh together.

His comedy night was a huge success and clips of his jokes and us laughing were shown throughout the actual TV show. Harley didn't use our differences to make us laugh at each other; he cleverly used what we have in common to keep everyone laughing.

The other three people involved, Sam, Dee and Jason who were amazingly strong people, are all in wheelchairs for different reasons. When Harley joked, "The only one who can walk is the one without any legs!" We all cracked up at the irony without anyone feeling disrespected.

Mum and Dad were in the audience too and they laughed along with everyone else, which is especially funny because their English isn't great so I'm pretty sure they didn't understand most of the jokes but were caught up in the energy and atmosphere of it all. Nothing makes you laugh like laughter hey? It was a memorable experience that I am so grateful for.

∿∿∿

My exposure on *Taboo* also created another opportunity when the producers of the show contacted me to say a disability support group from Darwin wanted me to speak at a disability

CHAPTER 7

conference up there. Sam from the TV show was asked too and we made the most of the opportunity.

I felt privileged to be involved as part of a panel where the audience asked questions all about us and our personal perspectives and experiences of living as a disabled person. We also had the honour of meeting Dylan Alcott, the incredible Australian Paralympian who was a special guest speaker at the conference too.

I was so happy to have the freedom of hiring an unmodified car and driving Sam and I around to see the sights of Darwin and Litchfield National Park. I didn't realise how tiny Darwin is compared to Sydney but they have a fabulous night market at Mindil Beach, which puts on beautiful blazing sunsets almost every night over the Timor Sea.

After that trip I could feel my life was really gaining momentum and I didn't want to stop learning or looking for opportunities. I was really opening up to new ideas and branching out to new horizons.

I was always looking for personal development but now I could see the benefit of understanding business and personal opportunities in line with my vision, my story and my growing philosophy to make a difference in people's lives. Whether it's in the gym, meeting them on the street or speaking on stage.

With that thinking in mind I went along to a Tony Robins

Success Resources event, which was a memorable day full of buzz and energy. It also gave me the chance to listen to other speakers such as JT Foxx, an outspoken entrepreneur who made a big impression on me talking about his methods for business networking and if I'm honest, growing wealth as well.

Foxx explained a good point about credibility by association. If I were to connect with the right people, not only in Australia but also around the world, then I would have a greater reach to share my story and so touch thousands if not millions of people around the world.

The gym will always be my first passion however I don't just live for the moment like I did before the accident. Nowadays I set myself paths and priorities from a wider perspective. I began to work towards gaining financial options and opportunities to ensure a safe financial future.

It was a big decision but I was so intrigued by Foxx's idea around brand association and networking that I booked my first trip travelling alone (just me and my legs) to his coaching workshop in Hawaii in July 2019.

It was a hefty investment in myself, future proofing because you can never know what might happen around the corner. Once again I was able to hire a car and it was the most surreal experience driving on the opposite side of the road. But it gave me an incredible sense of achievement being on such a beautiful trip all powered by my own steam.

CHAPTER 7

I was able to sit down one on one with JT Foxx for a short time and get some fast-talking business advice before moving onto other experts that help you in more detail. It was a great lesson in connecting with a wider circle and looking for opportunities further afield from where you live. It gave me the taste to find out more.

∿∿∿

You might assume the workshop would have been the highlight of my trip to Hawaii, I know I did. But like any good adventure story, the real highlight happened when I least expected it.

After the event was finished I wanted to explore the island and went on a short easy walk to Tantalus Lookout in Puu Ualakaa State Park. The high altitude of the open viewing platform made Honolulu a gorgeous sight to remember. The city in the foreground with the beautiful blue ocean reinforced what people say about this majestic island, you never want to leave.

Whilst absorbing all I could see through the lens of my camera, I noticed in the distance a volcanic crater. The sheer height of it compared to where I was standing only meant one

First hike to Tantalus Lookout where I saw the irresistible Diamond Head Crater in the distance.

thing, a better view of the city.

I picked out a friendly-looking tourist who was taking photos to ask her about the peak in the distance. She told me it was Diamond Head crater, another spot where many tourists hike to the top to see the breathtaking views of Honolulu.

Now I have to consider many factors when I want to do something new in terms of the environment so I asked her if she knew if the hike was disable friendly. She wasn't too sure so I researched on the internet and it looked promising, at

CHAPTER 7

least to reach a certain point. I couldn't resist heading there as my next spontaneous drive, only to be told by the National Park attendant that the walk *wasn't* accessible for disabled people — you can't always rely on Google I guess.

She was happy to let me through the gate though, "Just to look around a bit." But as I wandered around the base gazing at the shining sea and the enormous crater rising next to it, I looked up and felt inspired, invincible almost. I wanted to try and climb it.

∿∿

The hike was made up of semi-paved winding pathways, with tunnels and killer stairs heading up to its 500m elevation, a total of over 2.5kms. *Could I do it?* I wasn't sure but something compelled me to put one foot in front of the other and start climbing. I came equipped with a hat, sunscreen, water bottle, camera and my trusty walking stick to aid me in unfamiliar terrain.

I asked a local guide and they said that there was a lower point that I could reach to see the view, just before the stairs began. I thought, *Sweet; that should be smooth sailing to get to.* It all started fine, flat pavement with a bit of an incline, as expected when you're climbing up a crater. It started to get steeper so more energy was needed just to propel myself forward.

Did you know that a bi-lateral amputee uses over 200% more energy compared to an abled person?

Now you can picture my mental strength tackling the slope. Then the pavement ended and in came the rocky boulders. Yes, a sudden transition with unpredictable foot placements meant that even the experienced hikers could injure themselves. This strange terrain wasn't what I was hoping, why did nature have to be so uneven and … *natural?*

Either way, I reminded myself that I had been expecting a challenge so got down to business. The good thing was that there were handrails along the way, which I surely made use of, swinging my left leg over and onto each boulder while my right leg followed.

At this point, I was using a lot of upper body strength to help me take each step. Did I tell you the weather for this monumental climb? Fittingly it was an idyllic sunny day with wispy clouds across the sky. My face glistened with sweat and I had to keep up my fluid intake whenever I stopped to rest. I memorised the gorgeous sunny moments of the adventure in my mind.

Each time I felt tired another hiker would happen to shout out a word of encouragement or admiration, which would spur me on further. Actually it wasn't just when I felt tired,

One of the staircases making up the astronomical 327 steps of my climb. Photo credit Ichizo Kobayashi.

the fact that they saw me hiking up there by myself inspired them to throw out the excuse book of staying on the couch.

To know that by just being myself and not letting anything stop me from living life was making other people pause to watch my efforts, just shows the positive effect my story can have in and outside my peripheral vision.

∩∩∪

I knew I was doing something magical when a man approached me and introduced himself as Ichizo Kobayashi, the editor of a local magazine, *Wasabi*. Ichizo asked if he could join me on the climb. He had never seen someone quite like me on the trail and my mechanical swagger had caught his eye. He asked me if he could write an article about my adventure that day for his magazine. Naturally I said yes - all publicity is good publicity after all.

I now had a companion with me to watch my struggles as I finally reached that first lookout point that the local guide mentioned when I made my mad decision to climb. And I admit the view halfway up was amazing. I could have turned back then I suppose.

But I couldn't resist looking higher up to the real vantage

CHAPTER 7

point: the peak of Diamond Head crater. After all, people hiked to get to the top, not to hike halfway and settle for the view I was looking at. I looked beyond the trail to the stairs that came next.

It was my final day in Hawaii. I didn't want to leave the island with thoughts of what could have been. Following a quick deliberation with Ichizo, I decided to soldier on. Now technically these steps weren't as difficult as I had anticipated compared to the rocky boulders I had already encountered. However the total number of steps was 327, so all I can say is that it was damn tiring that's for sure.

I remember tackling the first flight of stairs, which then led into a small tunnel. As I finally reached the tunnel entrance, I noticed every hiker; at least 30 were standing to the side of the internal wall of the tunnel. They had noticed me inching my way up those demanding steps and chosen to wait for me to reach the top before congratulating and clapping me for the big challenge I was taking on.

A bi-lateral amputee on the cusp of completing Diamond Head Crater! I may have been the first to accomplish such a feat.

It was fun to have Ichizo's company along the way too and he gave me extra motivation. When you think you can't go on, it's good to be reminded why you're doing it in the first place. A few times as I struggled upwards, I asked myself, *why am I doing this climb again?* It was certainly a random act that was not planned when I had woken up that morning.

Maybe those tasty ramen noodles (a must-try in Waikiki) from that morning spurred me to adventure, or was I trying to replace my disappointment from the underwhelming aquarium that I had visited? I wanted to leave this place on a high note so I must have unconsciously been looking for a challenge. After all, everything happens for a reason.

Eventually I made it to the top lookout at 231m (761ft) in elevation. I was speechless with happiness as I embraced the stunning views around me. I can still feel the exhilaration from that moment whenever I look at the photos Ichizo took of me that day. If someone had shown me a photo of me on top of that crater seven years ago, I would have thought it was photoshopped - seriously!

I had reached an incredible pinnacle in more than one sense.

Khoa is sharing more in his INTERACTIVE book.

See exclusive videos, audios and photos.

DOWNLOAD it now at
deanpublishing.com/legless

Success. Photo credit Ichizo Kobayashi.

My Genium has stair functions but better to be safe than face plant. Photo credit Ichizo Kobayashi.

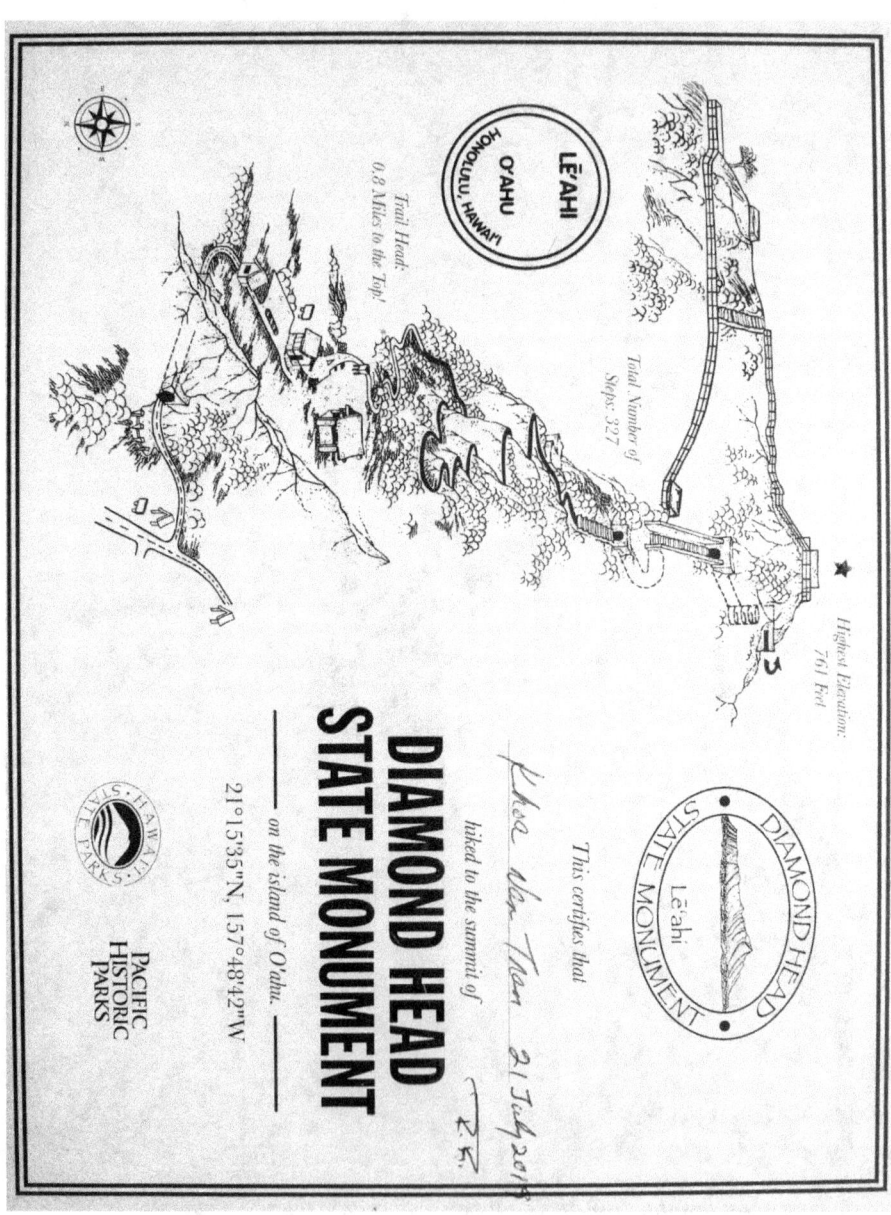

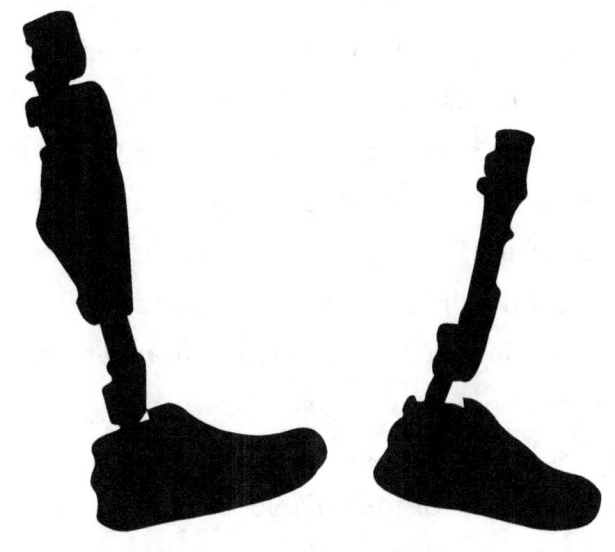

CHAPTER 8

LEGLESS TO LEGLESS

In the first few weeks and months after my accident, I never imagined the possibilities that would open up to me in the years to follow. I have lived a whole world of joy and adventure since losing my legs — a strange but true one. I have even pushed my new legs to their limits as one of my legs actually 'died' from so much use straight after my trip to Hawaii.

CHAPTER 8

When I arrived back home in Sydney, the step counter on my leg was off the charts. I also noticed it made an unfamiliar sound when it was charging. When I opened up the app that I use to activate different modes on my leg, an error message popped up notifying me to not use the leg; I had overworked it.

After six good years of service, my leg decided that enough was enough. My leg probably thought, *who in their right mind can make technology literally propel them back to freedom?* My metal legs just hadn't met someone like me yet.

Thanks *Ottobock*, for the reliable technology that enabled my physical journey. I have replaced my legs since then with the upgraded version, the Genium X3 from *Ottobock* and these ones are similar to their predecessor but are now also waterproof.

Theoretically they make my shower legs redundant I suppose, but I'm kind of attached to them from earlier times so they still have a place in my life. Otherwise I've never had to do anything in regards to my osseointegration.

It's been the most incredible example of technology and biology working together as one.

Once my legs were reloaded, in November 2019 I was ready to set off again. This time I was off to Los Angeles to attend the JT Foxx Mega Success Event.

People came from all around the world to learn about methods for business growth and also to meet the celebrities who came along as brand association opportunities. You never know who you might meet that could help your cause in the future.

It went for six days and was much more in depth than the workshop in Hawaii. It was at the Hilton Hotel in Anaheim California and I slipped into style by upgrading my tiny rental car to a convertible Camaro so I could look the part driving down those iconic streets lined with palm trees!

My first stop was Gold's Gym in Venice Beach. Yep, Arni's old hangout and the mecca of body builders everywhere. Just to stand where so many Mr Olympia had trained over the years was incredible. And it was a bit of fun standing next to my namesake, the Terminator in the LA Museum. It felt like meeting an old friend.

The Mega Success event itself was intense but so rewarding. The talks and seminars and guest speakers ran from 9 in the morning until 10 at night, it was pretty full on. I was actually in a bit of pain during that time because of the way I had been sitting on the 14 hour flight over there.

I had decided not to take my legs off and so my right leg had

Who wears it better?

been torqued at an acute angle for the whole flight. This had unknowingly applied a lot of pressure on my leg but it wasn't until the next day that I felt the full extent of the bruising. It wasn't serious but was really bad timing. I needed to keep my stick with me so I could move around the event comfortably.

It was a huge opportunity to meet and mingle with business minds and celebrities too. There were 2500 people there who had varying degrees of participation and involvement with the programs. The main purpose of the trip was to connect with the right people for your business purpose.

Olympic gold medallists Bruny Surin and Steven Bradbury – you gotta love a good underdog story.

My big moment on stage interviewing Jillian Michael. What a genuine and knowledgeable woman.

The action hero Dolf Lundgren: a gentle giant.

I was thrilled to interview Jillian Michael, a fitness trainer on *The Biggest Loser* US, in front of thousands of people on stage. I was a bit star struck and can't exactly remember our conversation but she was so excited about my passion for my gym and to learn that fitness had practically saved my life!

I met celebrity after celebrity; even *my* smile got a workout that day. Dolph Lundgren isn't always that Mr Bad Ass depicted on the big screen.

I also met the very special Unstoppable Tracy who was born a four-way amputee but has accomplished a string of physical and professional feats that blew me away. She was so smiley and positive I instantly connected with her.

I finished the event with so many connections, photos, stories and associations it was fantastic. My Facebook circle went crazy after this event. Not just with 'random' faces but also with the fascinating people who all went through the workshops together.

A huge highlight in LA was catching up with Ichizo! The editor and friend who I had met climbing Diamond Head Crater in Hawaii. He showed me around for a few days, checking out the millionaire mansions around Beverley Hills. I promised a friend I'd find JLo's star on the Hollywood walk of fame. Man, that walk is long! It took me 12 blocks to find it just to take a photo for my friend. Ichizo was a fabulous guide and helped make my trip so memorable.

Unstoppable Tracey: my *inspiration.*

I came home exhausted, happy and grateful for such a meaningful experience that will help me with my future options. There are countless people I am so thankful to for supporting me on my journey; their care for me has actually helped others too.

I've now heard of other amputees in similar positions to me, enjoying the benefits of osseointegration all thanks to the original efforts of my amazing case manager who didn't stop working and advocating on my behalf.

My journey hasn't stopped though; I am growing, learning and changing every day. A huge lesson for me has been not to hold onto the past. I have seen how past experiences can hold a person back from embracing their future. How people can carry the negative energy with them and wonder why they can't seem to move forward.

I knew I didn't want to do that; I wanted to do the opposite. Even before the accident I always tried to see each moment for its possibilities for light and laughter. This helps the shadows fade into the background where they belong.

This outlook helped me overcome each hardship in my recovery. Even if most of the situation appeared shitty, there

CHAPTER 8

was always at least one tiny spark of light and hope. I focused all my attention on making that spark brighter, blocking out anything that tried to hold me back, even if it took day after day, week after week of being patient.

Like when I was learning to walk with my robot legs. I knew I had to be on crutches for a while and so I didn't give myself a time limit on how long I should use them for. I just focused on those small moments of progress. As small as just taking one step after another until slowly over time, I realised I only needed one crutch with minimal pressure applied to the ground to support me.

Just like being in a gym pumping iron, I knew with repetitions, my aim would grow closer. In that case, grow with confidence to ditch the walking aids, stand tall and walk off independently into my future.

∽∽∽

Since the great personal success of my trip to Hawaii, I've been balancing many passions in my life. I love the challenges of running my gym even in this new, unknown, post-pandemic world. One of my favourite things I am grateful for is being able to get up early to open up for members who prefer

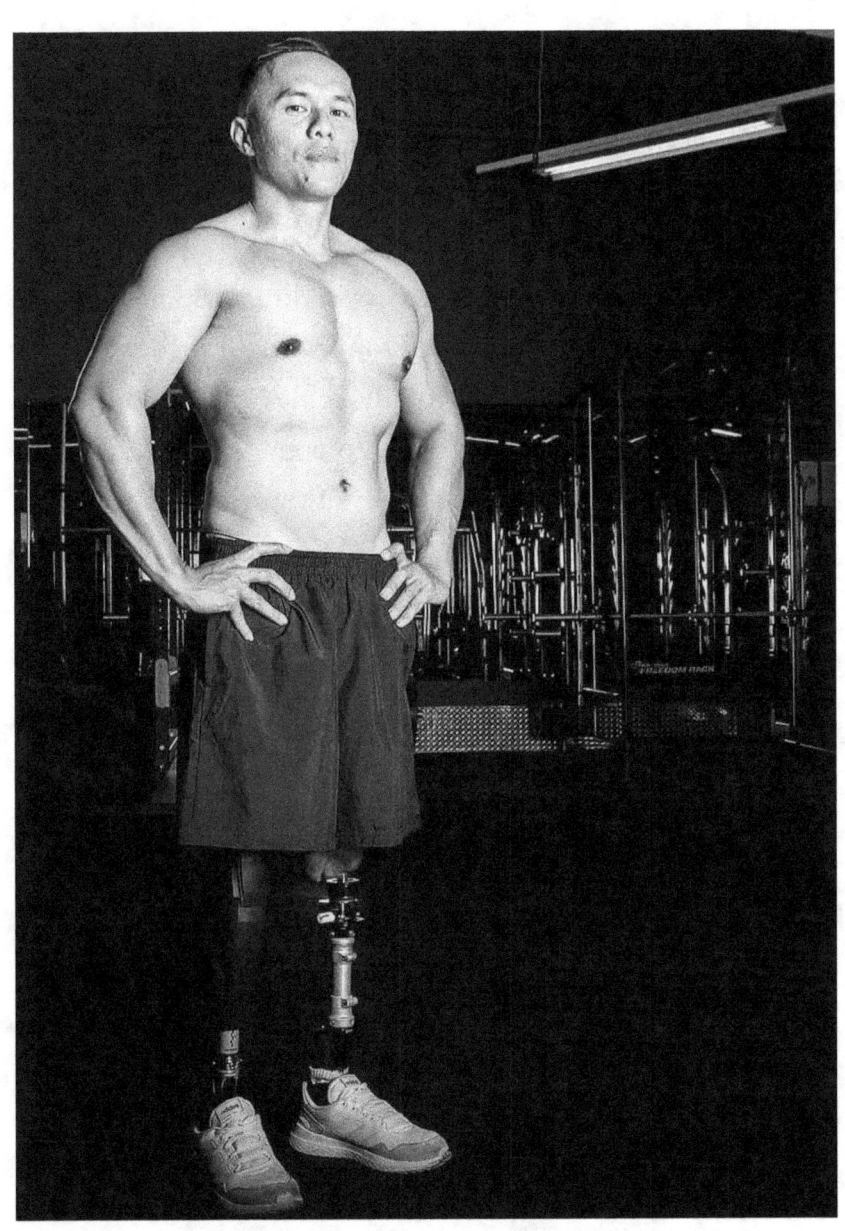
That time I was eating chicken breast and broccoli. Photo credit Helen Tran.

CHAPTER 8

to come in at that time.

Despite recommendations from our Head Office to only open for a short window of time in the middle of the day, I thought it was the right thing to do to offer earlier and later hours. We can't necessarily cover the wages for doing that, but for me, giving them access in difficult times is more important than costs so I said, "Don't worry, I'll cover it."

Don't think the idea is totally selfless of me though, I hope it might tempt more people to come along and secure their loyalty to our great gym: a bit of return business that'll pay off down the track.

Along with my new head for business, another surprising element to my life now is the spiritual awakening I've experienced as I continue to embrace the possibilities that I connect with in my life.

For example I'm involved in a Spirit Mind Awareness (SMA) enterprise and can use my love of IT to create videos helping to get the message out to the masses. Our messages include all sorts of topics encompassing wellness, meditation and mindfulness businesses; after all Spirit overflows into everything in our lives. One day we hope to make SMA a staple in universities and general teachings everywhere.

I would never have thought about all this before the accident. To give you a concrete example of what I mean, my beloved Skyline that I bought so many years ago and lovingly

Photo credit Helen Tran (*owe you one sis*).

CHAPTER 8

modified and converted, has been sitting like a prized museum piece in my front yard for years waiting to be given a new lease on life.

You can imagine I had been dreaming of restoring her again for many years. I was going to install a duck clutch to allow myself to drive a manual and relive some former glory. The 'runs' have had to adapt to this modern world and while the rev heads still meet up in car parks to admire each other's handiwork, actual street racing is a pretty risky thing to still be into.

I hear them rev their engines from my office or I hear the burnouts a couple of hundred metres away from the creek I used to cross. All that open space is a shopping centre nowadays. Listening to the cars, I think how much I'd love to be there. My next thought is, *No way, it's too cold!* I'd rather stay tucked up in bed!

I still love the old Skyline but it's time to pass her over to someone who can actively look after her. I might donate her to a Facebook forum group whose aim is to take on big car projects to transform them. I could watch the whole process online as they bring her to life once again, how rewarding would that be!

Before you think I've left my love of machines and speed behind completely, I also make time to go to the racetrack a few times a year when the weather is cool and I can test myself against the clock.

I'm only racing against my own skill and time, the best type of test. Each time I race I am grateful to have been given the ability to slip behind the wheel, push my foot to the floor and feel my heart rate skyrocket as I fly around the tight corners. Sometimes I feel my old buddies are right beside me, laughing with Khoa and his cool robot accelerator legs.

Sometimes my legs help me get noticed more. Like the time I was at a Ferrari festival and the mechanics in the pit garage saw me looking longingly at the cars behind the rope and so they invited me into the garage to get a closer look. I can't say no to an opportunity like that!

You have to be fearless on the track.

CHAPTER 8

Or I was pretty impressed when I entered a selfie competition with a cut out of the Supercars driver Aaron Russell that won me tickets to Bathurst 1000 in 2015! I have to make my look work for me sometimes, ha ha!

The flipside is also pretty cool too. Sometimes I'm working out at the gym and afterwards people will start chatting to me about the workout when they look down and get a shock, "Man, I didn't realise you don't have any legs!" How great is that! Disability doesn't mean you *can't* do, you just have to figure out your own way so you *can* do.

∿∿∿

I feel so much happiness in whatever my day brings. It could just be sharing a laugh with a colleague or client at the gym or enjoying the creative process of making SMA videos with messages of spirit and love that connects us all.

In fact, another light bulb moment came when I realised the spiritual principles I have discovered in recent years, were actually things I had been subconsciously practising at the gym already; actions and beliefs around support, community, love and giving.

I love the happiness in a person's eyes when I help them

reach a certain fitness goal, or the joys that come from fostering a sense of community where everyone feels welcome and connected. I don't do my job for the money. I do it for the light it brings into my life and to return that light to others.

I like to keep my business brain in top gear by delving into the complexities and potential of Forex trading in order to have financial options in the future.

I love connecting with people when I share my experience and listening to their own unique stories too. I really enjoy speaking on stage as part of belonging to the Speakers Tribe in Sydney. This has opened up more opportunities than I could have imagined.

Mum's home cooked Bánh xèo is still something to be grateful for, as was my first live concert which Adele conveniently scheduled on my birthday so 95,000 people could celebrate with me - what can I say, I'm popular.

What a ride it's been looking back on my escapades since the accident. Writing this book has been both sobering and heartening, as I've relived my adversity and achievements throughout my life. It has helped me reflect clearly on the events and choices that have shaped who I am today. While they may have seemed impossibly hard at times, they have empowered me to feel truly free in my life today.

I know to expect the unexpected too; I recently developed an infection in my stump, which I ultimately had to go to

CHAPTER 8

hospital for. Don't see it as a setback my friends, I was happy to brighten up the sad faces of the hospital staff!

My wound needed a debridement procedure (thorough cleaning), which involved going into theatre. I always challenge the anaesthetist to see how high I can count before I black out on the table. I reached 16 that day - a record! I think you know I'm a little competitive with myself by now.

Munjed and I still joke around too. When he came in to see me before my recent stint in theatre, he looked at my stump all covered in sterile bandages and pretended to be shocked, "Oh no, what happened to your leg!"

I laughed back, "I wrapped it up for you as a surprise!" If there's a joke to be made, I say make it!

I did learn my lesson though. No more cleaning on my hands and knees. This was out of routine for me and most likely caused the infection; I'll just delegate all cleaning from now on — nice one!

Getting through the trials of my recovery means I know I can overcome anything else that may come my way. Each day brings a new challenge; it's an ongoing process. But now, I know I am good at finding the bright thought in each moment.

For example, if I have to go into hospital again, I think how much fun it is to cheer up the new people I meet there. If I have trouble finding the energy to start an exercise session, I remember how my fitness was my saviour when my life was in jeopardy that fateful night. It motivates me to keep at it.

Just like me, each of you reading this has unique strengths that can pull you through those inevitable hardships in life. If it feels hard to find your own strengths sometimes, here are the simple lessons that have been so effective in moving me forward; I hope they can help you too.

ACCEPT QUICKLY

Time we cannot reverse so why dwell on the past?
Live in the present so your focus should not be
on - would've - could've -should've - instead
use your high vibrational frequency for *I will*.

FORGIVE EASILY

It may be hard to let go of someone else's sins if you
were at the receiving end of them but trust me, forgiving
is one of the most powerful tools mankind has in our
power because in the end, you wouldn't want to
have them living in your head rent free.

BE FIT

Being physically active is one of the reasons why I'm still here today. I truly believe that my sustained lifestyle back then of regular sessions to the gym and mountain biking, actually counteracted the excessive liquor I devoured day in day out so keep your heart pumping and strong!

APPRECIATE EVERYTHING

Before my amputation, I never realised how incredible the human mechanism is. The saying is true; you don't know what you've got until it's gone so look around and appreciate everything the way it is right now. Celebrate every little, tiny step you take, it all adds up to your destination. Be grateful for each moment of progress in your life.

DISCOVER YOUR POTENTIAL

Even though I lost my legs, I never imagined the potential I would have with these robot legs. Who can say they can grow taller as they age? I can! Don't limit your thinking. When the unexpected happens, new doors open up to you and you'll begin to see endless possibilities. Where there's a will, there's a way!

In the end remember to:

BE HAPPY AND STAND TALL!

"What will you do next Khoa?" I hear you ask.
There are too many possibilities to list them all - except one.
"Keep smiling!"

ACKNOWLEDGEMENTS

I would like to thank all the people that helped me grow, figuratively and literally. Thank you to my family and friends who were there for me when I was at my lowest. Without their support and listening to my bad jokes, I might have been tempted to think about a different life that could have been ... *living on a yacht on the Caribbean Sea eating a canapé array of seafood whilst basking in the sun* — BRB — finding a time machine 😊.

I would like to thank the crew who saved my life at the crash site, and the doctors and nurses who performed my life saving surgery, their extraordinary commitment and skills I am forever grateful for. Thank you Munjed and the team, whose expertise and love helped me get back on my feet.

I would also like to thank all the wonderful people I have met since the accident; they have inspired and helped me so much. They have opened a new world to me, surrounded by the spirit of possibilities and opportunities. I am so excited for the potential of the future (you know who you are) ... and that will be a whole different story.

ABOUT THE AUTHOR

Khoa Nam Tran knows what it takes to beat the odds. Since losing his legs in a car accident in 2012 at the age of 29, Khoa has embraced his new life following two osseointegration procedures that not only resulted in his much-loved robotic legs but also an incredible sense of freedom and thirst for life.

Khoa has become an inspirational speaker to thousands, appeared on television and radio programs as a voice for the disabled in the community and spread his entrepreneurial wings far and wide.

Acceptance, gratitude and exercise are Khoa's founding principles for living a fulfilled life and he practises positivity not just every day but every moment. He happily shares his story to help people overcome their obstacles and give them hope for when the unexpected happens.

Khoa's spiritual journey continues through his studies into Spirit Mind Awareness and incorporating a holistic approach to running his successful gym in Sydney; helping people from a place of pure love.

He loves spending time editing videography and photography and exploring new business ventures. You can often find Khoa pushing his limits around the racetrack where focus and clarity are paramount to keep moving forward.

www.khoanamtran.com

TESTIMONIALS

'Out of all the people I know without any legs, Khoa is definitely one of them. Actually he's quite possibly the only one, but then again most of my friends wear pants so it's hard to say. The thing that's most impactful for me about Khoa is not his trauma or his tenacity or his ability to stand on his own two feet ... it's actually just him. Simply Khoa. Khoa on his own is just a beautifully positive passionate person ... a true rarity in today's world, and I'm all the better for knowing him. I endorse this with everything I have. Get involved on the Khoa joy train in any way you can!'

HARLEY BREEN
AWARD-WINNING COMEDIAN AND HOST OF TV SHOW *TABOO*

'Khoa Nam Tran is a captivating storyteller. In *Legless to Legless* he takes his readers on an emotional rollercoaster and sprinkles it with humour. When he first stepped on stage at Speakers Institute, his genuine and down-to-earth character instantly shined through with his contagious smile. His resilience to fight all odds and turn any bad situation into a positive one shows what we are all capable of when life throws a curveball and delivers an unexpected plan. Khoa is a very powerful speaker. His story simply must be heard.'

SAM CAWTHORN
FOUNDER OF SPEAKERS INSTITUTE AND SPEAKERS TRIBE
ENTREPRENEUR | AUTHOR | SPEAKER

TESTIMONIALS

'Khoa is an amazing person. He lives a life without limits and he literally stands tall without legs. *Legless to Legless* is a great read for those who are ready to be inspired to live life to the fullest and to be motivated to soar high in life!'

DR CATHERINE YANG
AUTHOR OF *STEP ON FEAR*

'Khoa is one of the most inspirational, radiant, positive-minded and hilarious humans I've met. His incredible true story *Legless to Legless* demonstrates how the right attitude and perspective in life, even when you've been thrown big challenges and obstacles, makes a big difference. Khoa keeps it real and gives his readers a master class on how to use the transformative power of positivity to live a full life.'

RITA BARBAGALLO
AUTHOR OF *MAGIC AND MIRACLES*

'Having known the challenges of adversity myself, it was inspiring to read Khoa's book *Legless to Legless* and see a fellow human being that embraced and understood the power of acceptance, gratitude, humour and positivity. His ridiculously resilient attitude can help everyone stand tall and create a motivated mindset to overcome obstacles and achieve.'

JESS VAN ZEIL
AUTHOR OF *EYE WON: POWERFULLY POSITIVE AND RIDICULOUSLY RESILIENT*

ENDNOTES

1 *The State of the World's Refugees, 2000: Fifty Years of Humanitarian Action.* (2000). Switzerland: Oxford University Press, pp 87-90.

2 Icare. 'Lifetime Care and Support Guidelines and Policies.' icare.nsw.gov.au. Retrieved October 13, 2020. https://www.icare.nsw.gov.au/injured-or-ill-people/motor-accident-injuries/guidelines-and-policies#gref

3 Network 10. *Taboo*. Episode 4 "Physical Disability" (Aired 21 August 2018 13 June 2019). https://10play.com.au/taboo

~ To Tonee and Becca ~

Always part of the story

Peace and love

Khoa

www.ingramcontent.com/pod-product-compliance
Lightning Source LLC
Chambersburg PA
CBHW071615080526
44588CB00010B/1146